MOVING OUT!

**Practical stuff
you need to know
when you**

MOVE OUT
of HOME

ANNI GRIMWADE

RampallionPress

WHAT OTHERS ARE SAYING

"Full of tips you won't find anywhere else. I would definitely recommend it."
Emily Drew (19) Melbourne.

"Essential for anyone leaving home. It's a must-have even for those who think they know everything!" William Brookes (21) Melbourne.

"There's not much you need to know when you first move out of home that isn't in this book." Penny Lafferty (25) Sydney.

"Pack this book along with everything else when you leave home. You'll need it!"
Josh Lord (23) Perth.

"A great resource for young people moving out of home for the first time, and an excellent support for those already living independently."
Dr. Emily Horwill, Clinical/Health Psychologist, Melbourne.

Published in Australia by
Rampallion Press
PO Box 1111, Elwood VIC 3184
www.movingoutbook.com.au & www.rampallionpress.com.au

First published in Australia 2014
Copyright © Anni Grimwade 2014

National Library of Australia Cataloguing-in-Publication entry has been applied for.

Grimwade, Anni
MOVING OUT!: Practical stuff you need to know when you move out of home

ISBN: 978-0-9925928-0-6

Cover design by Sherwin Soy
Layout and design by David Schembri Studios
Editing by Amanda Spedding, Phoenix Editing
Printed by Griffin Press
Typeset in Palatino

Disclaimer
All care has been taken in the preparation of the information herein, but no responsibility can be accepted by the publisher or author for any damages resulting from the use of information contained in this work. Professional advice should be sought for individual problems.

Readers may note this book has been written in Australia and therefore some details may not be applicable to readers from everywhere.

DEDICATION

Moving Out! is dedicated to my three reasons for writing it:
Hannah, Archie and Hamish.

It is also dedicated to Tim, the only person I'd like to be an empty-nester with.

ABOUT THE AUTHOR

Anni Grimwade started professional life as a physiotherapist in Melbourne before becoming a management and productivity consultant in Sydney. After completing her MBA at Stern Business School in New York and moving to Hong Kong, she worked as the general manager of a recruitment company and subsequently as a university lecturer and programme leader before the handover of the colony to Chinese rule in 1997.

During a 5-year stay in Jakarta she undertook freelance editing work, and then returned to Melbourne with a growing family where she was able to resume a range of management consulting assignments. She has an Applied Science degree in Physiotherapy and an MBA in International Business.

Throughout these different careers, she has baked furiously, qualified as a wedding cake decorator, opened a holiday sewing school for teenagers, become the spreadsheet queen of budgeting for family and friends, and cleaned her house begrudgingly. She is quite good at French, not too bad at Indonesian and tries her hand at speaking 'Teenager' as well.

Anni lives in Melbourne with her husband Tim and three teenage children, none of whom listen to her. She will give them each a copy of this book.

ACKNOWLEDGMENTS

My grandmother always said to count my blessings, so here they are: Gretta Blackwood, Martine Browell, Caroline and Marcus Cottrill, Rhonda and Blair Denys, Niki Dimopoulos, the East Malvern Ladies' Mahjong Club (EMLMC), Fred Grimwade, Joan Grimwade, Lisa Grimwade, Martin Grimwade, Steve Grimwade, Rebecca Imbrosciano, Marianne Kagiaros, Sophie Kempton, Kara Lowe, Samantha Macansh, Julie Postance, Archie Roberts, Hamish Roberts, Hannah Roberts, Tim Roberts, the Rouse-Griffith Thank Tank, Dave Schembri, Amanda Spedding, Jenny Thompson, Pru Thompson, Thursday playgroup, and of course, Donald Ward.

Thank you to you all.

CONTENTS

Introduction

I first moved into my own place when I was 20. The time felt right and I was keen to spread my wings so I moved out with some friends from uni who, in hindsight, I didn't really know all that well. We enthusiastically rented a dodgy A-frame house with a terrible layout, and moved in with high hopes.

After a few weeks, things started to fall apart. My flat-mates didn't know how to cook, none of us had any interest or skill in cleaning, and we each had different expectations of what it meant to live together. It was a long year by the time the lease ended. We battled to get our bond back as a result of an over-the-top party that destroyed the carpet, and it was a difficult time for all of us. I went home, tail between my legs, richer for the experience but at least Mum was happy to see me!

A few years later I moved out again. My best friend and I rented a sweet little house in Carlton and it was one of the happiest times of my life.

At that time we didn't have anything much to guide us, so with those early misfortunes in mind and a few years of experience managing a house and family I have written this book. I hope it will help you move out of home successfully, first time around.

Anni Grimwade
Melbourne

December 2014

CHAPTER 1

A PLACE TO CALL HOME

Unless Great-aunt Mabel has left you a fortune or you were a teenage dot-com billionaire, you will probably have to rent your first home when you move out. You will be thinking about how great it will be to get away from your annoying little brother or sister, and how your parents won't be there to tell you to tidy your room. But there are a few other things to think about as well, so read on.

Haven't Got Time To Read The Whole Chapter? Read This.

1. Moving out is expensive! In addition to the rent, add up the cost of the bond, moving expenses, furniture and utilities and be amazed

2. A lease is a legal contract. Once you sign it, you can't change your mind

3. Choose your flat-mate carefully. Make sure you know them well and have similar lifestyles

4. Establish the ground rules early on. At a minimum, work out how you will share money, cleaning and food

5. Get your own contents insurance – the landlord (owner) won't cover your computer or other valuables, even if there's a leak from upstairs.

Can You Afford To Move Out?

Moving out can be expensive. It's not just the weekly cost of renting your dream home, but there are a lot of other expenses as well. Make sure you consider the costs of:

- The bond (four-six weeks rental cost)
- Removalist fees (or thank-you pizzas if friends are helping)
- Furniture
- Kitchen utensils, crockery & cutlery
- Bed linen and towels
- Appliances (e.g. fridge and microwave)
- Cleaning equipment
- Residential parking permits
- Electricity
- Gas
- Internet
- Water (if applicable).

CASE STUDY: THE REAL COST OF RELOCATING

Now that Julia has finished uni she's determined to move out of home. She works out a budget and after finding a flat for $410 a week, and allowing $100 a week for utilities, feels comfortable that she can afford it on her take-home salary of $700 a week. What really surprises her is the cost of relocating – over $2300 before she even has her first night away from home. This includes her bond ($1640), moving costs, and the purchase of a TV and microwave as well as a couple of items from an op shop to supplement the furniture she's getting from her family. She decides to delay moving out for a couple of months till she has this money saved up.

Lesson: Living away from home costs more than just the weekly rent

Moving budget

Truck rental for half a day $50
Bond $1640
TV $350
Microwave $199
Vinnies: bedside table, coffee table,
bookshelf & TV stand $90
TOTAL: $2329

Preparing To Move Out

Finding a flat-mate

Be careful about your choice of flat-mate! There's not much worse than living with someone you can't stand (unless you marry them as well), so this is definitely not the sort of decision to make at the end of a big night out. But think about it carefully and you can end up with someone who is a joy to live with.

A good co-tenant will be someone who:

- You have known for some time, or at a minimum is a good friend of a good friend. Some people find success on the Internet, but you can't really be sure about what you're getting till it's too late
- Can be relied upon to contribute financially. Even if you are a model tenant, if they are late paying the rent, YOUR credit rating may be affected. This might not matter now, but when you are trying to borrow to buy a house you may get turned down
- Will contribute to the running of the house or flat – the cleaning, the shopping and the general maintenance
- Has the same hours as you – not a night shift worker when you like to have friends around for breakfast
- Has the same habits as you – if you are a neat freak and they like to live in a bomb site it will only lead to unhappiness
- Feels the same way as you about smoking, alcohol and illicit drugs
- Is similarly social – if you love a big chat at the end of the day and your co-tenant wants to be left alone, this can cause friction
- And has similar feelings about ethical issues. For example did you grow

up on a cattle farm and your flat mate is a vegan? Do you feel strongly about the environment and your flat mate thinks that all greens are loonies?

CASE STUDY: THE PERFECT FLAT-MATE

Simon was excited about moving into a place of his own but was having trouble finding a flat-mate. All his friends seemed to be moving home or going overseas so he was delighted to hear of a friend of a friend who was keen to move out and wanted to live in the same area. They met, and although Gemma seemed a bit quiet, it all seemed to go okay. When Gemma moved in, Simon was slightly concerned that she didn't seem too communicative and went into her bedroom and shut the door straight away.

Over the next few weeks it became clear they had different ideas about living together – Simon was keen to socialise together or at least have a bit of a chat, but it seemed Gemma spent most of her time in her bedroom with the door shut. She wasn't interested in sharing food or household tasks and when she did come out of her room, was stoned most of the time. It became worse when she began to be late paying the rent and Simon had to cover for her. In the end, when Gemma mentioned she had a friend looking for somewhere to live, Simon jumped at the chance and moved out.

Lesson: Think about whether you and your flat mate have similar lifestyles and are looking for the same sort of living arrangement

Laying down the ground rules

Before you move in, you and your co-tenant(s) need to establish the ground rules. Some people like this all clearly written down and stuck on the fridge, while the idea of this freaks out others, but either way it's good to establish:

- What date you will all pay the rent. If you are paying separately, real estate agents and landlords prefer the rent to all be paid on the same day, not in dribs and drabs
- How you will manage cleaning the house or flat. Will you have a roster, or will you have dedicated tasks (e.g. you do the bathroom, I'll do the vacuuming)
- How you will manage food in the house. Will you have a kitty that you put a specified amount into each week for supermarket shopping? Or, will you each have your own food?
- How will you pay the bills. Will you have a kitty? Or, will you divide each bill as it arrives?
- How you feel about 'special friends' sleeping over, and how often is okay? What about one-night stands? (This is important due to security issues)

- How you will manage Internet usage so that it is fair on everyone?

Finding somewhere to live

The best place to find somewhere to live is on the Internet – there are lots of good websites around but two good places to start are *RealEstate.com*, or *Domain.com*. If you are gay or lesbian and looking to share, go to the Gay Share website. In all these websites you can register for free alerts about places that are likely to suit; this will save you spending even more of your life on your computer! Be careful moving into a flat belonging to a relative. You won't get a rental reference, and if things go wrong it can sour the relationship.

It is likely there will be a number of people interested in the same place, so if it looks competitive, the following process is recommended:

- Find somewhere that you are interested in
- Put in an application (yes, before you've seen it). This does not oblige you to rent the property
- When you go to the 'open for inspection', introduce yourself to the agent and say that you have already put in an application
- If you can, use a parent as a guarantor. Agents will always look at your rental history and until you have one, they are going to see you as something of a risk. Having a parent as a guarantor will make them more likely to rent to you and will still mean that over time you gain a rental reference

Checklist: A good place to live

- Will be on the first floor or above if it's a flat and not on the ground floor. This is particularly true for girls, as ground floor flats can offer poor security
- Will have good street lighting. You should feel comfortable coming home alone at night
- Will have a secure entrance
- Will have rooms oriented well. In the southern hemisphere, north-facing will give you sun through most of the day; east will give you morning sun; west will give you hot afternoon sun, and south may be dark
- Will have adequate parking. If there is no car park provided, is there adequate street parking or even better, residents' parking on the street?
- Will have suitable immediate surroundings. Perhaps there is a club round the corner that will have late-night noise? Or a train station or freeway within hearing distance? Maybe there is a beautiful park across the road, or a beach just a short stroll away?
- Will have appropriate rooms. Can you live with the condition of the carpets or the kitchen and bathroom? Is that tiny little bedroom really going to be suitable?
- Has potential. Perhaps the flat would be great with a coat of paint. Check first that it's okay with the landlord then go for it!
- Will have adequate heating, and if appropriate, cooling.

Once you have signed your rental contract, if you find out that something is not to your taste it is too late. You can't get out of it.

Lease Arrangements

Remember that leases are legal contracts, so should not be entered into lightly. Take home a copy of the lease before you sign it and don't be pressured into signing on the spot. These contracts are generally quite generic and are based on a standard set by your state's governing body, but you should read yours thoroughly, and ask your family to read it too. If there's something that is not clear to you, ask the rental agent for clarification. You cannot change your mind once you have signed the lease because you misunderstood the meaning of a particular clause.

Types of lease

There are two types of lease: one is for a fixed term, with a set ending date (this may or may not roll over to a monthly lease); the other type is a periodic agreement for no set period and with no set end date. Beware the latter arrangement as it may mean you need to vacate at any time with just 30 days' notice.

Whose names are on the lease?

You need to decide whose name (or names) will be on the lease. If you are sharing, it is most likely that you will have a 'co-tenancy' arrangement – this means that everyone who is sharing will have their name on the lease, and everyone will share responsibility for payment of the rent and the condition of the property. If one of the co-tenants moves out, they are still responsible for the property until their name is removed from the lease, even if they are long gone. Be careful.

Sub-letting is rarer. This is where you just have one name on the lease, and then that person allows others to become sub-tenants. It means you have control over who lives there and can get them to leave relatively easily if needs be. But a big drawback is that it's ONLY YOU who is responsible to pay the rent or to keep the house in a reasonable condition, even if you are sharing with several others. You must advise the agent or owner if you are subletting the house but this should not be a concern as they are not able to refuse your application without a valid reason.

Paying the bond

When you sign a rental contract, you will have to pay a sum of money that is held over until the end of your lease. This is called a 'bond'. It covers:

- The cost of repairing any damage that has been caused to the house, whoever did it
- Any cleaning that needs to be done once you leave
- Replacement of any items which belong to the landlord
- Unpaid rent
- Bills that you should have paid but which are now left for the landlord to pay.

Depending on the level of the rent you are paying, the bond will generally be between four-six times the weekly rent, so it can be substantial.

Bonds are held by a third party, not the rental agent, and are returned to you if all is well. Remember that the bond will be returned to the people listed on the bond lodgement form, so if you take over someone's spot in a house, make sure that you contact your real estate agent to get the form changed to reflect this.

CASE STUDY: BONDS ARE SERIOUS

Will moved into a house with two friends, Emma and James. The rent was $600 a week, and the bond was four weeks' rent, a total of $2400, or $800 each.

During the three years they lived there, Emma moved out and Jenny moved in. Time was tight on the day they all vacated so they did a quick tidy and a bit of a clean and jumped ship. Will was moving home before going overseas and because he knew he'd be getting bond money back, he spent the expected $800 on a new phone – he put it on his credit card.

A few days later, he was horrified to find that the real estate agent wanted to keep $1500 out of the bond money – $200 for cleaning, $800 for replacing the carpet in a bedroom where some red wine had been spilled, and $500 for a new washing machine they all thought had belonged to Emma but which they actually saw on the Condition Report had belonged to the landlord. The bond they finally got back was $900 or $300 each. Will couldn't afford to pay off his credit card bill and was stuck with a $500 debt.

Lesson: Bonds are serious. Look after your rental property

Condition report

When you go to collect the keys to your new place, the agent will give you a Condition Report. The agent will have completed it and you, as the tenant, should go through it very carefully once you get back to your rental property, and fill out anything the agent has missed. Get on to this quickly as it's a bit like a carton of milk – it goes off quickly and you don't want to have to go and get a new one.

Don't include maintenance items such as broken handles or blown globes as these will be repaired during the time of your tenancy. (But do make sure you tell the agent so they can be repaired). This next point is important so listen up!

Take photos of any damage the agent has missed, print off the photos in colour and then attach them to the report.

When you move in, the real estate agent should give you a list of their preferred suppliers, which you should stick on your fridge and make a copy for your own reference.

Rent payment

While it can differ from agent to agent, it is likely that you will need to pay your rent once a month, in advance. Generally you will pay electronically, but the agent is also required to accept cash if you are behind in your payments.

If you are sharing, choose one date every month that is rent paying day. This makes it easier to sort out should there be any issues about whether payment has been made, and it will make your agent happier. Even if you are a model tenant, if anyone sharing the house is late in paying, your rental history is also affected.

Keys

When you collect the keys, make sure you get a photocopy of the form confirming the number of keys and remotes you have taken. Most agencies will do this and it will save problems at the end of the tenancy. Normally you will get one key per bedroom but you can ask the agent to cut extra keys or you can do it yourself.

Another thing – don't lose a security key! It can be tricky to get extras cut so a replacement might cost you up to $80 per key.

Pets

While it can be a little bit more difficult to find a place that allows pets, it's not impossible. But make sure your co-tenants know about your pet and never have a pet as a sneaky co-tenant. You do know that dogs can destroy gardens and puppies can destroy carpets so how about a fish or hermit crab?

Preparing To Move In

Insurance

The landlord will insure for legal liability (e.g. if a guest breaks their leg falling down the stairs) and also for fire and flood damage to fixtures and fittings. This will cover flooring, lights and ovens, but will NOT cover your belongings. So if there's an overflowing sink or a leak from above that wrecks your computer, it's not their responsibility. Get your own contents insurance!

Did you miss that? Get your own contents insurance! There are a number of companies that will insure the contents of your apartment/house for theft, fire and flood, or even just your belongings if you are sharing (e.g. all the motoring associations around Australia) and this can cost as little as $5-10 per week. Search 'renter's insurance' and you can take it out on-line.

You have two choices here: just insure your own belongings or insure the whole house/apartment's belongings (i.e. yours and your flat-mates'). I recommend that you just do your own – it can save a whole lot of grief later. It means you can insure for an amount you determine, and you can decide how much excess you want to pay (that's the part you pay before the insurance company kicks in) and you decide which items to include.

If you do decide to insure your flat-mate's belongings and yours together, remember that anyone who has their name on the policy can make changes to it. So your flat-mate can change the address of the policy (so you don't ever get any correspondence), can increase or decrease the value of the policy or the excess payable, or they can take your name off it completely.

What's included in my rental?

You'll need to think about what furniture and appliances you'll need when you move in. You should write a list for each room, detailing what you need and where you'll get it.

There are some things that you won't have to worry about, as for every rental property, the following items will be included:

- All fixtures and fittings such as blinds, flooring and light fixtures with working light bulbs (although you will need to replace them once they blow)
- Smoke detectors
- Oven and cooktop but generally no other white goods, although this is not always the case.

What I need to move out:

Kitchen
Fridge – the spare one from the garage
Microwave – buy new
Table – Uncle James' old one
Oven - supplied

My Bedroom
Bed – the one from my bedroom
Bedside table – from Vinnies
Cupboard - ? maybe from Mum
Mirror - ?

Second Bedroom
Desk & Chair – from my bedroom
Bookshelf – from Vinnies
Rug – the old one from the garage

Living Room
Sofa – from the spare room
Coffee table – from Vinnies
TV – buy a new one

Connecting utilities

When you rent a property you will find that it comes without any electricity, gas, phone, Internet or water. Connecting the first four (electricity, gas, phone and Internet) will be your responsibility, while connecting and paying for water may be either the landlord's responsibility (if you are in a block of flats and there is only one water meter) or your responsibility (if it is a house, or a flat that has its own water meter).

There are two ways to connect your utilities. You can do a bit of an Internet trawl to work out which service providers will give you the best value. A comparison website such as iSelect can help. Then you call them individually to get the connection process started.

Alternatively, an easy way out is to get a connection company to take care of it for you. You can still specify which provider you would prefer (although getting the best deal might be trickier) but there is no charge to yourself and it is extremely easy. There are several companies out there (enter 'connection utilities' into your Internet search engine) – one example is *Direct Connect*.

A couple of things to remember:

- Think about whether you want a landline. Apart from your parents, the only people who'll use it are dodgy people wanting to 'fix' the terrible virus on your computer and charities seeking donations. It's old technology and you won't use it much – consider not having one
- If you decide you do want a landline, consider getting a ban on mobile, STD (regional) or ISD (international) calls. This can stop bills getting out of hand and disagreements further down the track
- Don't sign up for a phone or Internet plan that is longer than your rental agreement (e.g. don't sign up for a 24 month Internet plan when your rental agreement is only for 12 months). And be aware of the amount of download that a share house can use – LOTS!
- Make sure the names on the utilities match the names on the lease (i.e. don't put your name alone on the electricity bill, as then you have a legal responsibility to pay it, not your co-tenants).

What time can I move in?

Make sure that you confirm with the agent what time you are wanting to move into your rental property. Many apartment blocks have specified times to move in or out, particularly on weekends. This is in order not to disturb the other tenants.

Changes During Tenancy

Changes to the tenants

If you finally get rid of that nightmare flat-mate and someone new is moving in, both the old tenant and the new one must sign a Lease Addendum removing the old tenant from the lease and adding the new one. This will need to be signed off by the agent and the landlord.

Note to self – the part of the bond belonging to the person leaving will not be returned. Bonds only come back at the end of the lease, so the new tenant will have to pay the old tenant their part of the bond.

Rent increase

The landlord can't increase the rent during a lease. At the end of the lease period, they can increase the rent but must give you 60 days' notice by normal and registered post, and this can't happen more than once every 6 months.

There is some room to negotiate the amount of a rent increase and if you feel what they have decided is unreasonable, you have nothing to lose from (politely) ringing the agent and requesting the landlord consider a smaller increase. If you get nowhere and really think it's worth up-scaling the protest you can apply for a hearing with the tribunal in your state:

- *ACT & SA Residential Tenancies Tribunal*
- *Northern Territory Consumer Affairs*
- *Queensland Residential Tenancies Authority*
- *Tasmania Consumer Affairs and Fair*
- *Victorian & NSW Civil and Administrative Tribunals*
- *Western Australia Department of Commerce/Consumer Protection.*

Further information is available on their websites.

When Something Goes Wrong

Problems with the property

Consumer Affairs Victoria[1] defines urgent repairs as:

- A burst water service
- A blocked or broken toilet system
- A serious roof leak
- A gas leak
- A dangerous electrical fault
- Flooding or serious flood damage

- A failure or breakdown of any essential appliance (e.g. for hot water, water, cooking, heating or laundering)
- Failure or breakdown of the gas, electricity or water supply
- Any fault that makes the premises unsafe or insecure
- A faulty appliance that causes lots of water to be wasted
- A serious fault in a lift or staircase.

You should contact the agent immediately by both email and phone if you have problems in these areas. (Phone because it's quick; email because you will have a written record of the problem and when you contacted them).

If it is not during working hours (and it never is!), you should advise the agent by email and then contact the appropriate repairer from the list that you put on your fridge when you first moved in. (You did do this, didn't you?) Agents and landlords are not happy if you contact someone from the Yellow Pages. You are entitled to have repairs such as these fixed within 24 hours. For non-urgent repairs you should also advise the agent in writing and these will be done over a reasonable timeframe.

Problems with your co-tenant

First of all, please tell me you followed the advice (Finding a Flat-Mate and Laying Down the Ground Rules) above?

Okay, but things have still gone wrong. First of all, don't worry! It will all work out.

If you are unhappy living with someone, it's most likely that they are having issues with you, too. It sounds easier than it is, but try to have a low-key chat. Explain what issues you are having with them and see if you can come to a solution. As always, it's better to broach small issues as they arise rather than sitting on them until they become huge problems.

If, after all your efforts, this doesn't work, you can also try dispute resolution (services are offered by such places as the Tenants Union of Victoria, or Community Justice Centre in NSW) but both parties must attend so it can be tricky.

If it's clear that you can't sort out your problems, tell your co-tenant that you will moving out as soon as you find someone to take over your part of the lease. Once you find someone, both you and the new tenant will have to sign a Lease Addendum with the agent.

If you can't find anyone to take over, unfortunately you will have to grit your teeth and bide your time until the end of the lease, telling your co-tenant that you will be giving notice to the agent 28 days before the end of the lease, and if they wish to continue staying in the house, they will need to find someone to take over your position on the lease.

In a worst-case scenario, you can apply to have your lease terminated by the governing body in your state (see earlier in this chapter) but you will need to have a serious reason, not just that you didn't get along.Remember that if you are co-tenants, you are both responsible for any payments due and for the condition of the house, so try to sort out any issues of this nature early on. Whatever happens in the house will also reflect on your tenancy report.

Eviction

Rest assured that this doesn't usually happen! But this time it has. Oh dear.

Non-payment of rent

Eviction is most usually for non-payment of rent but can also be for maliciously causing damage, or endangering other people, as well as using the premises for illegal purposes. You will be given 14 days' notice to vacate by normal mail as well as by registered mail. If you do not do so by the specified time, the matter will go to the governing body. Clearly you should avoid this.

Noise

With regards to noise, remember that not everyone wants to party until 3am, so if you are being too noisy, you will be given three successive notices then the matter will revert to the relevant governing body as above. Be careful – this will affect your tenancy report and you will miss out on a good reference for future rentals.

Unclean rental property

While you are living in your rental property, you will have to endure inspections. The agent will have a good look around (though just at the surface – they're not going to go all weird and go through your cupboards) and then will complete a report that gets sent to the landlord. Remember that there are rules limiting the number of times an agent can come through per year and how much notice you need to be given, so it can be wise to check the regulations in your state. You can get evicted if your place is very unclean, so make an effort!

If you are falling down in this area, the agent will write to you with a Breach Notice and give you 14 days to remedy the situation.

End Of Tenancy

So, you've come to the end of your tenancy and you are all going your separate ways. Don't forget to hand in your notice (the agent will have advised you of the period required, usually between 14-28 days), otherwise the tenancy will just roll over from month to month. And remember that you were paying your rent in advance? That means there is no payment due when you move out. Yay!

If there has been any damage, it can be quite easy to fix. For instance, you can replace a hinge on a cupboard, or spot clean a stain on the carpet yourself. Once you've done what you can, make sure the place is really clean, take photos, and then return the key to the office. Don't assume the agent has a key and don't be late – if you are you will continue to be charged rent day by day. The agent will do an inspection which you should attend if you can and then will do one of two things:

1. Return the bond (well done, you excellent tenants!)

2. Ask you for agreement that part or all of the bond be retained to do repairs. Both you and the agent will complete the relevant form confirming your agreement.

If you and the agent can't agree, the agent will need to apply to the appropriate state governing body to get them to decide if a portion of the bond should be withheld.

Once the bond (or part of it) is returned, leave a forwarding address with the agent and say adios to your co-tenants. Happy days.

Five Top Tips

1. If you don't have a rental history, see if your parents will act as guarantors. Happy landlord, happy real estate agent, happy you!

2. Put your list of the agent's preferred repairers as well as your utility suppliers on the fridge. Don't lose it, as that'll be the day the power goes out

3. Don't sign up for a landline or Internet plan that is longer than your lease (e.g. a 24 month Internet plan on a 12 month lease)

4. Use a connection company to connect your gas, electricity and water

5. Keep your place clean. Yep, you can get evicted if it's too dirty.

With many thanks to Rebecca Imbrosciano for her help in writing this chapter.

CHAPTER 2

SERIOUS FINANCIAL STUFF

Your parents said it would never happen, but you've moved out and have managed to get yourself a job. You feel great seeing your salary come into your account and so you should – it's a big step towards standing on your own two feet. Congratulations!

When you start earning there are a few things you need to know about banking, loans, investment and more. It's all here in this chapter. It might seem boring, but people, it's useful, so grit your teeth and get stuck into it.

Haven't Got Time To Read The Whole Chapter? Read This.

1. A credit card uses money that you borrow from the bank; a debit card uses your own money from your own account. Credit cards are therefore more risky than debit cards, as you can build up debt very quickly. Pay off your bill at the end of each month or else you will pay daily interest of more than 20%

2. You should save as much as possible and borrow as little as possible to avoid paying interest to the bank. If you do have to take out a loan, work hard to get the lowest interest rate you can and pay it off as quickly as you can

3. Some companies pay dividends to their shareholders that have franking credits attached. These may help to lower your tax bill

4. You need to lodge a tax return if you are over 18 years old and earn more than $18,200 a year, or if you have had any tax taken out of your salary

5. If you die without a will, your assets will be distributed according to a legal formula rather than according to your wishes.

Banking Basics

Bank accounts

You may have had a bank account since you were a little kid but this may not be appropriate for you now. Most likely your bank will recommend the following three accounts:

1. *A transaction account*

This is your everyday account – your salary will get paid into this and you'll withdraw cash from it to fund your groovy new independent lifestyle. Check around the banks until you find one that has no fees. You won't want to keep your savings here because there is generally no interest paid on these accounts, so you will need...

2. *A savings account*

This is an account that earns interest and it's where you can put your monthly savings as well as that nice little birthday cheque from Auntie Mavis and your prize money for winning Tattslotto.

Your interest rate is likely to be low (just a couple of per cent), although the banks will always offer you more to start with to lure you across. You can also get higher interest if you open an incentive saver account and then make at least one deposit and no withdrawals each month.

Be clear about why you have this account – perhaps it's to pay for a deposit on a house, or for a car but make sure you understand about compounding interest (see further on in this chapter). You won't want to be withdrawing from this account very often.

3. *A Visa or MasterCard debit card*

These operate off the transaction account. They are not credit cards but mean that you can use the money in your transaction account to shop on-line or wherever a credit card is accepted.

To set up a bank account you will need 100 points of identification tallied up from any of the following: a Medicare card (25 points), your driver's licence or social security card (40 points for the first, then 25 for each subsequent), a passport or birth certificate (70 points), a social security card (40 points) or a utility bill, credit card or bank statement (25 points each)[2].

It can be useful to have all of your accounts with the one bank as it is easier to manage (just one App or website with one PIN to navigate), but don't stress about establishing a relationship with your branch. Bankers are rational people (read: not suckers) and they won't be more likely to give you a housing loan just because they've seen your face once a week for a couple of years. Given that banks are so ruthless, make sure you are ruthless back and look around for a bank that offers accounts with no fees.

Internet banking

Make sure you set your accounts up for Internet banking when you open them, and then be sure you know how to do two things: transfer funds and access statements. You should also download the App for your bank – it will make banking so much easier and you'll probably end up using this more than Internet banking itself.

Don't worry about getting statements by mail as in most cases these are easily accessed on-line whenever you need them, and particularly at tax time. And while we're talking about on-line banking, don't discard purely on-line banks as they can be very competitive when it comes to interest rates as they're not paying for outrageously priced offices in the CBD.

Cheques

A word about cheques – don't bother! Cheques are on the way out and are mainly used by old people (like your parents). According to the Australian Payment Clearing Association (APCA), the number of cheques used dropped by 37% over 4 years, from 437 million in 2006 to 276 million in 2010[3]. They're dinosaurs.

PINs and passwords

PINs and passwords are really valuable bits of information so treat them with respect! They can provide access to your bank accounts, your phone, shopping accounts and all sorts of stuff. Make sure you have different passwords and PINs for all your log ins.

CASE STUDY: A LOST WALLET AND MISERY

Like everyone, Victoria found it hard to remember all her PINs so used her birth date and month for all her cards. She was pickpocketed while she was at the cafe at uni but only realised that her wallet was missing when she returned home an hour later. By that time, both her savings account and her transaction account had been emptied. The thief had simply found her birthdate elsewhere in her wallet and used an ATM to access all her hard earned cash.

Lesson: Don't choose an obvious PIN

When you choose a four digit PIN, make sure you don't use your birth day and month (DDMM) or birth month and year (MMYY) – if you lose your wallet, any idiot can get these from your licence and access all your accounts.

In addition, of 3.4 million PINs analysed by Datagenetics[4], three PINs accounted for 20% of the total. Three! Isn't that unbelievable? These PINs are 1234, 1111 and 0000 so clearly these are out too. Numbers in the high 1900s are popular as well, so avoid your birth year, and 2580 is used a lot as it's straight down the middle of the phone keypad. (Look at the Datagenetics blog – it's a weirdly fun read). Most people prefer even numbers, so try one that ends in an odd number.

When it comes to passwords, the longer the better. Use a mix of numbers, symbols and upper and lower case letters, and if you can avoid using an actual word, so much the better.

Issues, of course, arise with trying to remember all your different PINs and passwords. Be smart and use a programme or App to help. PC Magazine has done a review of password managers so if you're starting from scratch, have a look[5]. Alternatively, ask your friends what programme or App they use – personally, I like 1Password[6]. Don't be tempted to write PINs down – and NEVER, NEVER, NEVER write them on the back of the card. Did you hear that? Even disguising them in the middle of a phone number is the oldest trick in the book and therefore very unsafe.

What is a BSB number?

Sometimes you'll need to provide a BSB number. The BSB number stands for Bank–State–Branch number. The BSB is usually used in association with an account number, and together they form the complete reference to a specific account. You may need this when filling in forms.

(And if you're interested, the first two digits generally refer to the bank, the third digit is the state, and the final 3 digits are the branch. So for example the BSB 083-004 is 08 – National Australia Bank, 3 – Victoria, and 004 – 330 Collins Street, Melbourne. There you go.)

Tax file number (TFN)

A TFN is a unique number that helps the government keep track of your financial affairs, such as your tax and your superannuation. You only apply for it once, and you keep the same number for the rest of your life. You will need it to open a bank account, submit your tax return or make a tax enquiry, start a superannuation account, or when you start or change jobs.

If you are 16 years or older and are an Australian Resident, you can apply for a TFN on-line at www.ato.gov.au and then attend an interview at a participating

Post Office. You'll need to bring along proof of identity such as your birth certificate.

Treat your TFN as if it were a bank account number. Don't share it with anyone you don't trust and don't keep it in a place that can be easily accessed by others, such as in your mobile phone or in your wallet.

Direct debits

Direct debits are payments you set up with companies to allow them to take money automatically from your account to pay bills. They can be set up for a fixed amount (e.g. for a phone contract) or for a variable amount (e.g. for a power bill). If you want to switch banks, your bank is obliged to provide you with a list of your direct debits. Even easier, your new bank can do all the work for you and change them all across.

Direct debits are great if you are sure you can afford them. It can be a good idea to set them up so they synch with your salary payment. For example, if you get paid on the 15th of every month, get payments taken out on say the 17th. This means you don't have to worry about forgetting to pay a bill and then getting slugged with a non-payment fee or interest. Don't worry about the bank getting it wrong – it's unlikely to happen and you will get it refunded if there is an error.

If you are really disciplined with your money management, pay all your bills with your credit card and then auto pay the credit card each month. This will give you up to 50 days of additional interest on your savings while they sit in your bank account.

CASE STUDY: USING DIRECT DEBITS TO MANAGE YOUR MONEY

Hamish had his $45 phone bill to pay every month, as well as a credit card payment and his electricity and gas bills. He set up automatic payments with each of the suppliers for two days after his salary payment on the 15th of every month. Charlie, on the other hand, waited for bills to come in and sat on them for as long as possible before he paid them. But by the time they were due, he had bills amounting to over $200 – and his bank balance was down near zero. The outstanding amount went onto his credit card... so now he had a debt to carry forward, and next month had to try to pay it as well as his regular bills.

Lesson: Bill paying should be automatic and your first priority

---

Cards

What's the difference between a debit card and a credit card?

A credit card lets you borrow and spend the bank's money up to a set limit. If you don't pay back what you owe at the end of the month, you will be charged a very high level of interest. This gets added to the amount you owe. (Yep, easy to see why you should pay it all back every month).

A debit card is linked to your bank account and allows you to spend your own money. It will have the Visa or MasterCard logo on it. But note again – you are spending money that you have put into your account, not borrowing money from the bank. So there's no interest to pay on what you spend.

Both credit cards and debit cards can be used to set up a secure payment method such as PayPal for purchases over the Internet, and can also be used when you're overseas or when you want cash out of an ATM.

The lowdown on credit cards

Credit cards can be a useful way to manage your cash flow, to tide you over a dip in your finances, or for an emergency. They can also offer benefits such as free insurance on purchases. But they can also be high risk as you can spend way too much before you realise what you are doing, and they can be expensive as they have a higher interest rate than other loans. A credit card can be useful, say, if your fridge blows up; it's a really bad idea to use it to borrow money to buy a bigger TV. If you want that new 80" curved screen TV, do what your grandparents would have done and save up till you've got enough money to buy it outright. You have the option to pay for it on your credit card, get the insurance benefit, then have the money to pay the credit card bill at the end of the month.

To get a credit card, the bank will require your last two pay slips, and information on what you own, what debts you have, and your current expenses. They will check with an external credit agency such as VEDA to see your credit history, and whether you have kept up with your payments or defaulted on any borrowings. In short, banks just want to be sure you can repay the loan.

The banks get their money from credit cards in a number of ways, but there are two that concern you. Firstly, there is an annual fee you have to pay to have the card (unless it's bundled in with another bank product such as a home loan), and secondly, there is the interest rate you pay on your purchases. At the time of writing, interest rates on cards varied between 12% and 20% (just as an indicator, home loan rates at the same time were around 5%). You do get an interest free period each month, which you should take advantage of, but make sure you repay everything you have put on the card each month, otherwise you can start paying hefty interest charges. In all cases, interest rates on cash advances (where you get cash out from your credit card and are in fact borrowing money from the bank) are ALWAYS very expensive and there is no interest free period on them. (Confused yet? Read on!)

Also, with many banks, any payments you make on a credit card will come off purchases first, and cash advances later regardless of whether the cash advance was made before or after the purchase, as these have a higher interest rate and are therefore more lucrative for the bank. So if you have $80 worth of purchases on your card and $20 worth of cash advances, and you make a payment of $80, the bank will pay off the purchases first. You will therefore still owe $20 for a cash advance at the higher interest rate.

So, how do you manage your credit card? Do one of two things: pay off your credit card bill in full each month, or even better, don't use your card at all. Keep it out of your wallet (some people store them in the freezer – sounds weird to me). Make sure that you keep your PIN secure. And watch out for late fees. If you can't pay off the full amount, pay off as much as you can – this will reduce the interest you'll be slugged. And don't ever use your credit card to pay off your credit card – this is like crazy, dude, and you'll just end up paying interest on your interest.

CASE STUDY: PAYING OFF YOUR CREDIT CARD

Zoe had just got a credit card and was having a great time with it. She got her first statement and was surprised to see she had spent $350 in her first month. She hadn't planned very well and couldn't pay it off, so at the end of the next month, she saw on her statement that she had been charged $7 interest as well as a late fee of $20. She had also bought another $125 worth of stuff, so now she owed $502.

At the end of the next month and $100 of spending, she again didn't quite manage to make any payment, so now she owed $602, plus $13 interest and another late payment fee, a total of $635. She was horrified to see how quickly the bill had crept up and quickly set up a payment plan with her bank so that there was a small automatic deduction each month.

Within 4 months she had paid off her bill, and from then on paid it off completely each month

Lesson: Always pay off your credit card completely each month if you can

Store cards

Some companies (particularly car companies and large furniture companies) will offer you a store card at an attractively low rate (even interest free) for a set period such as 18 months. The way they make their money is that after that time limit has expired, the interest rate will skyrocket to around 27% and you can get into all sorts of trouble if you can't pay the debt off immediately. The other problem with store cards is that they can limit you to shopping in the one spot. Unless you are extremely disciplined and will put the money aside to pay back at the end of the interest free period, avoid them.

Interest Rates

Interest is the amount of money expressed in a percentage that you either pay when you are borrowing money (e.g. a car loan at 6%) or lending money (e.g. a deposit with the bank at 2.5%). People watch interest rates (particularly those on loans) because they can make a big difference to the total cost of whatever they are buying.

> ### CASE STUDY: INTEREST RATES
> Sam and Rob are both borrowing $300,000 to buy a small apartment of their own. Sam has been careful with his credit history and hunts around, finally accepting a loan at 4.8% from an on-line bank. Rob has had a few defaults in his past and can only get a loan at 6%. Over 25 years, Sam will pay a total $215,697 in interest. Rob on the other hand will pay $279,870, a difference of $64,173.
>
> *Lesson: Interest rates and credit history matter*

Loans

Personal loans

Personal loans are small loans (well, in comparison to a housing loan) that you take for something specific such as to buy a car or to pay for a holiday. You will fill out an application either at the bank or on-line; a credit check is completed where they will look at your credit history then make a decision. Where a personal loan is better than a credit card is that the interest rate is often slightly cheaper (at the time of writing, around 9-10%, compared to up to 20% with a credit card).

Housing loans (or mortgages)

For most people a house is the biggest purchase they will ever make, and therefore the loan to buy it will be the biggest too. This might seem a long way off but bear in mind a couple of things: the bigger the deposit you have saved, the smaller your loan will be and the less you will pay to the bank in interest. You should aim to save at least 20% of the value of your house as a deposit; if you do not have the 20%, the bank will make you pay Lenders' Mortgage Insurance (LMI), a one off payment to protect them in case you default. This can amount to tens of thousands of dollars. But if your parents agree to act as guarantors, the bank may not require you to take out LMI.

Housing loans generally have a lower interest rate than other loans, so any extra cash you have should be spent paying off these other loans first, then your housing loan later. As with a personal loan, to take out a housing loan you will need to fill out an application, but the bank will be rigorous in looking at your past income to see if you have the capacity to repay the loan. Your budget (see page 50) will be useful here.

Lay-by

Okay, so lay-by is not really a loan, but it is a way to buy something when you don't have the ready cash. It is getting less and less common, but lay-by is still offered by some big retailers and it involves them putting away something you want to buy while you make payments on a regular basis until it's paid in full. There is a very small administration fee (usually a couple of dollars) but the best bit about lay-by is that there is no interest. Yay! The bad bit is that you don't get your item till you have paid it off (usually up to three months for clothes and consumer items) and if you change your mind you will have to pay a termination fee.

Credit Reporting

As you develop a history of payments, including credit card repayments, rental payments and loan repayments, you will develop a credit history. If you default on your phone, gas or water bill, this is where it gets reported. If you later apply for more credit, a report on your history (a credit report) will be accessed by the bank, which wants to establish how likely it is that you will run off to Brazil with their cash. You do not want to have a bad credit report, so work hard at repaying when required. And remember that if your name is on the bill, you are responsible for its payment.

New legislation relating to Comprehensive Credit Reporting[7] means that reporting will change from exclusively concentrating on the negative, to reporting the positive as well. This means that if you have paid off a loan successfully, any future lender will be able to see this on your record. Cool.

If you want to get a copy of your credit report, you can contact an organisation such as *Check Your Credit* or *My Credit File* on-line and provide them with some information that will allow them to identify you. This will include your name, date of birth, current and previous addresses, driver's licence number, details of your employer, as well as an official document that has your address on it, such as a rates notice.

Don't be sucked in by some of the websites offering to check your credit report for you for a fee: you do not have to pay for a credit report unless you want an express service.

Investments

Savings

You know that saving is an important skill to learn if you want to buy things and avoid hefty interest charges. But did you know about the joys of compounding interest? This is where interest compounds (or adds onto itself), which can make your savings increase exponentially. Say you decide to deposit $100 a month into an account. The interest paid will be as follows:

First month: Interest is paid on the initial $100

Second month: Interest is paid on the initial $100 + on the interest that was paid in the 1st month

Third month: Interest is paid on the initial $100 + on the interest of the 1st month + on the interest of the 2nd month

And so on.

So, over time, and if you make regular deposits, you will find the interest being deposited each month will be more than what you are depositing yourself.

CASE STUDY: COMPOUNDING INTEREST

Matthew gets his first job at 20, and decides to put $100 a month into an account that he won't touch till he retires. He contacts his bank and sets up an automatic deduction for the day after each payday, and because it comes out automatically, he doesn't actually miss it. At 5% interest over the 50 years in which he pays in $100 a month, his deposits total $60,000. However, the interest he has earned is a whopping $207,977.

Lesson: Take advantage of compounding interest

Shares

When you buy a share you are buying a part of a company (e.g. BHP) and becoming one of a whole lot of owners of that business. These shares are traded on the stock market so you can buy and sell your part ownership to other people. As a shareholder, you will receive information from the company including the Annual Report, which will help you get an idea about how the company is faring.

You buy shares for several reasons: one is because you hope the value of the whole company will increase and so your shares in that company will be worth more (and you will become a squillionaire). You can easily check the daily price of your shares on-line, and a good place to start is the Australian Stock Exchange (ASX) website. Multiply the share price by the number of shares you own to work out what your total holding is worth or join MyASX to set up a share watch list. On MyASX you can also play share market games and get market updates.

You also hope the company makes a profit, which will then be shared with you as a shareholder (a dividend). This generally happens twice a year, unless the company is not making a profit, in which case you will get nothing. When you first buy shares, the company will send you a form asking for your Tax File Number. Make sure you return it otherwise they will take out withholding tax from each dividend payment. You will also get a form asking you where you want your dividend payments paid. You should return this with details of your bank account. The alternative is to be sent a cheque, which can be dodgy – you have to make a special trip to the bank or ATM to deposit them unless they go astray in a pile of papers at your house first.

A third reason to buy shares is that they provide diversity in your investments so you are not having 'all your eggs in one basket'. Most people who hold shares will have them in a number of different companies, e.g. 10 or 15 organisations across a number of industries.

Some shares provide dividends that have franking credits attached. These are a way for the government to avoid taxing you twice on the same money (i.e. the company pays tax on their profits, then you pay tax on these profits again when you declare your dividend in your tax return). Franking credits can help reduce your tax bill so it's worth finding out if the shares you are looking at buying have 'fully franked' dividends.

If you don't need the cash, you can choose to reinvest your dividends in purchasing more shares in the same company, and in this way your investment will continue to grow exponentially. Just make sure you keep good records of the date of the reinvestment, the number of shares you 'bought' and the cost per share on that date – all this information is available on your dividend statement which is available on line or via the mail.

If a company is listed on the ASX, you will need to buy shares through a broker – be it an on-line one (such as Comsec or E-Trade) or a broker in an office. The ASX website can help you find one.

Shares are traditionally, over the long term, a better investment than either cash or property. However, there is always a risk with shares that their value will decrease and the higher the amount that you might earn, the higher the risk.

The ASX has excellent tools on their website under the education tab, including on-line classes, videos and tutorials and it's a very good place to start if you are at all interested in the stock market. They also have an excellent publication called Getting Started in Shares which you can download[8].

Superannuation

Superannuation is a savings system set up by the Federal Government where your employer sets aside money for your retirement. Yes – it's your employer who pays money into your super fund! When you start a new job, your employer will ask for your Tax File Number (see page 34) and for details of your superannuation fund (if you have one) so they can start making the necessary payments into it. If you do not have a fund already, you can nominate which super fund you would like to use.

Your employer must currently pay at least 9.5% of your salary into your super account every year, with this amount remaining at that level till 2021 and then increasing to 12% by July 2025. The managers of your superannuation fund will invest the money on your behalf (although you can nominate which way you'd like your funds invested) and this can be held as cash or put into shares, managed funds, and/or property. You will receive a statement every year from your fund detailing the value of your account.

If you can manage them, it is a very effective long-term savings strategy to make extra payments into your super fund. There are two tax benefits here: firstly, payments into your super fund are taxed at 15% which is likely to be less than your normal tax rate if you are on a reasonable wage. And then any earnings within the super fund are also taxed at 15%. Excellent.

But don't get carried away as this money will be tied up for many years and is not accessible unless there are extraordinary circumstances or a disaster, such as a terminal medical illness or death. The laws relating to super are complicated and ever-changing, but generally you will get access to the funds close to when you retire, and not if you get yourself into financial trouble.

Income Tax

PAYG

When you have a job, your employer will work out how much tax should be taken out every time you are paid, and they will send this directly to the government. This is called Pay as you go (PAYG). The amount of tax that is taken out of your salary depends on how much you earn. It's a sliding scale and the more you earn the more you pay (ranging from zero to 47% of your salary) and you also pay 2% of your income to the government to cover the cost of Medicare.

CASE STUDY: PAYG AND MARGINAL TAX RATES

Ned is finding it tricky to get the job of his dreams, and currently earns $35,000 a year doing part-time cleaning. He pays $3892 in income tax and Medicare, leaving him with $31,108 to take home. Every extra dollar he earns above $35,000 will be taxed at 19%, his so-called 'marginal tax rate'.

Claudia on the other hand has written a dating App that is going gangbusters, and is earning $300,000 per year. She pays the government $116,947 for tax and Medicare and takes home $183,053 each year. Her marginal tax rate is 47%, currently the top rate in Australia.

If Ned earns an extra $2000, he will keep $1580; if Claudia earns an extra $2000 she will only keep $1020 because of her higher marginal tax rate.

Lesson: the percentage of tax you pay changes according to your income

---

Tax-free threshold

There is a thing called a tax-free threshold – friend to the underpaid. This is the amount you can earn before you have to pay any tax. In the financial year ending June 2015, the tax-free threshold was $350 a week or $18,200 a year. When you start working with a company, they will ask you whether you wish to claim the tax free threshold with them. Make sure you only claim the tax-free threshold at ONE place or you will end up in a real mess.

> ## CASE STUDY: TAX-FREE THRESHOLD
> Archie was saving to go overseas and had his head down and bum up working at several jobs – nights at the local pub, days at Maccas, and weekends at a supermarket. By mistake he claimed the tax-free threshold at each of his three jobs so each employer took no tax out until he had earned $18,200 with them (a total of $54,600 for the 3 jobs). He got a huge shock at tax time as the Australian Taxation Office (ATO) sent him a bill for $9,292, which is the amount of tax payable on $54,600. Ugh.
>
> *Lesson: Only claim the tax-free threshold with one employer*

Lodging a tax return

Lodging a tax return is easy to do on-line – just get onto the Australian Taxation Office website and look up E-tax[9]. You will need the following to complete your return:

- Payment summaries from any and all job(s) you have held
- Financial statements including dividend statements from shares that you own, and bank statements
- Details of anything that you have used to earn income and the cost of which you may be able to deduct from your salary e.g.
  - Travel related to your work, but not travel between home and work
  - Charitable donations
  - Self–education expenses
  - Protective clothing
  - Home office expenses if you do some work at home
- Your Tax File Number
- Bank account details for payment of a tax refund if you receive one.

Tax returns cover a financial year running from the first of July of one year to the 30th of June of the following year (e.g. 1st July 2015 – 30th June 2016). If you submit your own tax return it must be completed by 31st October of the same year (e.g. 4 months after the tax year ends). You can also pay a tax agent or accountant to do your tax return, in which case the deadline will be later.

The ATO has a 'Do I need to lodge a tax return tool?' on their website but generally you will need to do a tax return if:
- You are over 18 and had income greater than $18,200
- You had dividends with franking credits (for an explanation, see earlier in this chapter) of more than $18,200
- You had any tax taken out of your salary
- You had a payment made into a superannuation fund by an employer
- You carried on a business.

What is a tax refund?

A tax refund is money the government returns to you (if you're lucky) after they process your tax return. Remember that your employer takes PAYG tax out of your salary throughout the financial year? When you submit your tax return, you will list deductions, which decrease your income, and therefore you will get some of this tax refunded to you.

Deductions you are able to claim on your tax return include costs relating to an investment such as interest paid on a loan to buy shares, or repairs to an investment property, franking credits for shares, and donations to charities over $2. (So be kind – it's win-win). You can also claim deductions relating to your work such as travelling from one place of work to another (but not from your home to work each day), stationery and other home office expenses, protective clothing and laundry.

CASE STUDY: TAX DEDUCTIONS

Maddie is working in the building industry on an annual salary of $40,000 and had PAYG tax taken out of $4547. When she did her tax return, she submitted deductions for protective clothing and travel of $2000 which dropped her taxable income to $38,000 which should attract a tax of $3897. Joy of joys – she received a nice little tax refund from the government of $650! This is because the deductions lowered her income so the tax she should have paid was less.

Lesson: Don't forget to think about what you can claim on your tax return

Your Will

No-one likes the prospect of dying but as difficult as it is to think about, it's a good idea to make a will. If you die without a will (i.e. you die 'intestate') your assets will be distributed according to a legal formula and not according to your wishes. This might mean that people you can't stand get everything and the ones you love get nothing. If you write a will, you can decide to leave everything to a charity, or to your best friend, or to your family.

The law is quite complicated in this matter, but generally if there is no will and you don't have a spouse or children, then it is your parents who will inherit should you die. If they are not around, then it is your siblings, and after that your grandparents.

When you make a will, you should get it signed by two witnesses using the same pen that you also used to sign[11] and date it. If it's a long document, the witnesses should sign each page. Remember that your will lasts until you die unless you revoke it, or you get married or divorced. In your will you should also nominate an executor, or person who is going to administer the will. They need to be over 18 years of age and someone you trust.

You can make a will on-line for as little as $20, or you can go to the legal aid website in your state for further information. As this is an important document, you should think about whether it might be better to get a solicitor to draft your will for you.

Five Top Tips

1. As soon as you open your bank accounts, download your bank's app. It will make all your banking quick and convenient

2. Don't use your birthdate as your PIN, or 0000, 1111 or 1234. And make your password as long as possible and include numbers and symbols

3. Treat your TFN (Tax File Number) as if it were a bank account number and keep it safe from prying eyes

4. Use compounding interest to your advantage. Set up automatic monthly savings now, and don't touch the money until you have reached your savings goal

5. Be aware of which deductions you are entitled to claim in your tax return to increase the likelihood of getting a tax refund.

With many thanks to Marcus Cottrill for his help in writing this chapter.

CHAPTER 3

MONEY, PERSONALLY SPEAKING

While it's important to understand the big picture when it comes to money, it's the little things that can make the difference. Ever heard the idiom 'if you look after the pennies, the pounds will look after themselves'? It's true: be careful with all your small money decisions, and you'll end up sitting on a pile of gold coins. Metaphorically speaking.

So, to make sure you and your money continue to have a harmonious relationship, read on. It could save you from lots of grief (and the horrible prospect of having to move home again).

Haven't Got Time To Read The Whole Chapter? Read This.

1. A budget is important. It doesn't matter whether you do it on-line, use an App, or scribble on a piece of paper, but you need to know where your money's coming from and where it's off to when it's heading out that door. A budget helps you work out where you really stand financially

2. You can work at keeping on top of things financially in a number of ways: increase your income, spend less on non-essentials, eat frugally, be economical at home, dress up for less, go out on the cheap, keep an eye on your banking costs and don't smoke. Ever

3. You can tell if a website is secure by checking if there is a little padlock next to the URL and that there are the letters HTTPS:// rather than just HTTP://. But I bet you all know that

4. Mobile phone plans from all providers are now required to have a CIS (Critical Information Summary). When you're looking at updating your mobile phone, the CIS will tell you what you're really getting into and let you compare one phone plan against another

5. If you buy overseas currency before you depart on holiday, you can be slugged with high fees, either at the bank or at the airport on departure. Withdrawing cash from an ATM at your destination is the way to go.

Budgeting

Okay, I'm not sure you'll like this idea, but one of the first things you need to do when you move out of home is set up a budget. This is a list of all the income you receive (such as salary, allowances, huge monetary gifts from your fabulously wealthy special friend or other payments) compared to a list of all the expenses you have (such as those associated with your house, going out, your car, new clothes etc.).

Why are budgets so important?

A budget is important because it tells you where your hard earned money is going, stops you spending more than you are earning and helps you think about where you might need to cut back. It gives you an idea of what your financial position really is, not just what it feels like and it helps you in forming realistic financial goals, both short-term (saving for that fabulous new pair of skis) or long-term (saving for a housing deposit).

When you first put together a budget, it will become clear how important it is to keep good records. A very simple and low-tech method is to put all your receipts and statements into a shoe box as they come in. These can include pay slips, phone bills, doctors' receipts, electricity statements, insurance bills, love letters etc. (No, not really love letters – I just wrote that to check you were awake). Until you manage to have a full year of all these papers and while you do your first budget, you will need to 'guestimate' some of the totals. A really easy way to keep a record of your spending is to use an App such as the Australian & Investments Commission's (ASIC) *Track My Spend*. It's free. Yay!

The tax year

Just to be confusing, the financial year (or tax year) is not the same as the calendar year. Being so clever, by now you've probably all worked out that a calendar year runs from the 1st of January to the 31st of December. Well, the financial year in Australia runs from the 1st of July of one year to the 30th of June of the next year, so you can choose whether you do your budget over the calendar year or over a tax year. It doesn't really make a difference.

How do I do a budget?

It also doesn't matter how you set up your budget, although using a computer spreadsheet means you can personalise it to your exact circumstances, it will do all your calculations for you and each year you can save annual copies which can help you see how your financial position is trending. (Hopefully better and better!)

A really excellent alternative is an on-line budgeting tool such as the one under tools and resources on the Money Smart website[12]. It is easy to use and you can export it into a spreadsheet. (This website is run by ASIC and has all sorts of handy information about money issues if you're interested. Have a play on it – you'll be surprised at what you can learn.) Most banks also have a budgeting tool on their websites so get on-line and have a look around.

But if this is all a bit heavy handed, even a piece of paper can give you a good start!

Sample budget

If you're a pen and paper type of person, here's a sample budget to photocopy and fill in. (Didn't your mother ever tell you not to write in books?)

My Budget	For the financial year:		
		Monthly	Annual
Income			
	Salary		
	Allowance		
	Other Payments		
TOTAL		$	$
Expenditure			
Household	Rent		
	Food		
	Takeaway food		
	Insurance		
	Electricity		
	Gas		
	Water		
	Repairs		
	Landline phone		
	Mobile Phone		
	Internet		
Education	Tuition Fees		
	Books		
Social	Going out		
	Presents		
	Clubs or subscriptions		

Car	Loan repayments		
	Registration		
	Insurance		
	Petrol		
	Servicing		
	Automobile Association		
	Electronic Tolls		
	Parking		
	Cleaning		
Other Transport	Public Transport Tickets		
	Bike maintenance		
Clothes	New Clothes		
	New Shoes		
	Dry Cleaning		
	Clothing Repairs		
Health	Doctor		
	Health Insurance		
	Dentist		
	Pharmacy/Chemist		
	Physiotherapist		
	Hairdresser, spa		
Pets	Food		
	Registration		
	Vet		
Other	Investment/savings		
	Super payments		
	Donations		
	Travel savings		
	Christmas		
	Emergency/ Contingency		
TOTAL		$	$
	NET INCOME MINUS EXPENDITURE	$	$

How to manage a budget

The aim of a budget is to end up with a bottom line that is 'in the black' – that is, ending up with money left over from an income that is greater than what you spend. If you find you have a negative bottom line and are 'in the red' (spending more than you earn), you will need to do one of two things: either stop eating (well, trim off some of your costs), or earn more income. Usually it's easier to spend less than to earn more, for instance, decreasing the number of takeaway meals you eat, rather than getting another part-time job.

You'll need to keep coming back to your budget. Don't think you are crap at managing money if it doesn't work out the first time – budgets need attention! They stop you running off the financial rails completely and will allow you to plan for rewards such as holidays, a car and ultimately, a deposit for your own house.

Good Money Habits

Okay, remember the bit at the start of this chapter about looking about looking after your pennies and the pounds looking after themselves? Well, here's the lowdown on how to put it into practice. All these habits will help you keep your budget in the black so have a read – there's 52 of them, so why not try one a week?

Getting more into your wallet...

1. Sell unwanted items on eBay or Gumtree. It's so simple even your parents could do it, and you might be surprised at what you can earn. Try books and branded clothes to start with

2. Get a part-time job

3. Offer to baby-sit or walk pets for neighbours

4. Offer to do something for friends that you do well (like fixing a car or ironing). Even if you don't actually get any cash, you can barter for something they can do better than you (like gardening or doing a budget).

...and taking less out of it

5. Do you really need it? If it's not something you will use a lot, see if you can borrow it e.g. DVDs from friends, books from the library, tools and cooking utensils from neighbours

6. When you're out shopping, tell yourself you can have that irresistible book, pair of shoes or piece of sporting equipment, just not today. Wait a couple of days to see if you might actually be able to live without it

7. Make presents for your family and friends (for ideas, look at the recipes in Chapter 6 of this book)

8. Find a bulk billing doctor (for an explanation, see page 118) – you will save around $30 a visit

9. Try to keep yourself healthy by eating well and exercising, and you can avoid pharmacy and other healthcare costs

10. Think about not having a landline. It's old technology and getting rid of it could save you over $500 a year.

Cheapskate eating

11. Make sure you go to the supermarket with a list, and stick to it

12. Make sure you know what is in your fridge before you write your shopping list, and try to plan meals so you use everything you have. Be creative and don't let food go off. There are websites that can help you – have a look at Big Oven[13] – just enter three ingredients you have in your fridge and it will give you recipes for them

13. Don't go food shopping when you're hungry – the theory is that you'll buy more

14. Buy home brands. Most of your basic unbranded ingredients (such as sugar, flour, butter, oil, tea etc.) are indistinguishable from branded items. Be more careful with choosing unbranded prepared foods such as biscuits and cereals

15. If you've done your budget (and of course you have!) just take the amount of cash you have allocated for supermarket shopping and leave your cards at home

16. Don't EVER buy water if you can drink the local tap water. Never. Refill a bottle and take it with you. It's like throwing money down the drain if you buy water and all those bottles will end up in land-fill

17. Make out you're at school again and pack your lunch. You can save $2000 a year

18. Think about not buying coffee when you're out. (Relax – I only said think about it)

19. Have a go at growing vegies at home. Tomatoes are a good place to start but if space and time is limited, try herbs

20. Cook at home, and avoid takeaway. Don't get into the habit of setting a routine such as always having takeaway on a Friday night. Make it 'soup night' or 'shake the freezer and see what falls out night'

21. Get to know the prices of things you often buy so you can tell where they are the cheapest

22. Buy non-perishables such as toilet paper and washing powder in bulk if you can afford to and have the storage space.

Being cheap at home

23. Don't leave appliances such as TVs and computers on standby; make sure you turn them off at the wall. According to Choice[14] – a wireless router can use over $20 a year in electricity, a multi-function printer can use over $23 and a DVR can be almost $60

24. Make sure you turn lights off when you leave a room

25. Put on or take off clothes instead of using heaters and air-conditioners

26. Shut windows and curtains, and use draught stoppers to avoid the need for air-conditioning and heating

27. Only do your machine washing when there is a full load, and use cold water

28. Don't tumble dry your clothes – it wears them out and the sun is free. If you don't have a washing line, use a fold up rack

29. Buy any household items you need at second-hand shops but only buy electrical goods if they have a 'safe to use' tag

30. If you want to buy something new, always check its price on the Internet first. You can then approach your retailer and offer them the chance to sell to you at the same price.

Dressing up for less

31. Buy your clothes from op shops. Celebrate your individuality – apart from the cost, an added benefit is that no-one will be wearing what you are!

32. Buy formal wear from eBay. Most items have only been worn once or twice and you can save hundreds of dollars

33. Get in to the habit of offering clothes you are sick of to your friends, and be happy to accept their offerings in return. This works well if you can find a friend with similar taste who is a similar size to you

34. Avoid buying dry-clean only clothes. It's expensive and who wants to have all those dodgy chemicals next to their skin? Check the care labels before you purchase

35. Learn how to hem and repair your clothes. Look in the *Clothing Care 101* chapter of this book or even get on to YouTube. It can teach you everything you want to know (and a whole heap you don't).

Entertainment on the cheap

36. Don't take your EFTPOS card with you when you go out at night. Use cash so you have to go home when you run out (but make sure you keep some aside for getting home)

37. Instead of going out for dinner, have your friends over for a 'potluck' meal – everyone brings their own drinks and a plate of food to share

38. Look out for free events such as concerts in the park and festivals, particularly in spring and summer. Your local council will have a programme on their website

39. Don't be pressured into spending to keep up with the people you socialise with – good friends will understand and if they don't, perhaps you shouldn't be hanging out with them?

Getting out and about without spending too much

40. Get into the habit of walking, running or riding your bike. You know it's good for you, good for the environment and saves your money. It also helps you to overcome compression garment envy by avoiding the gym

41. Cars are expensive. If you add up the purchase price, servicing, petrol, insurance and registration you'll be amazed. Maybe public transport might work for you?

42. If so, make sure you do your sums and work out which is the best type of ticket to buy. If you're not using it every day, you might find that it's cheaper to pay for individual rides than to fork out for an annual pass

43. If you are a full-time undergraduate student check to see if you can get a travel concession card

44. Remember how much fun it was when you car-pooled your way to basketball with all the kids in the back and Mum up front? Re-live your youth – see if you can organise permanent car pools for regular activities

45. And for one-off trips, see if you can grab a lift this time with someone going your way. Even if you don't have a car, as long as you have a licence you can offer them a lift next time. Check out a car share system such as GoGet[15].

Cheaper money

46. Make sure you save up for things you want to buy and don't want to borrow

47. But if you need to borrow, make sure you are ruthless in finding the best interest rate. Banks make money by loaning you money and charging you interest, so they want your business!

48. Try to go for a pre-paid phone plan so there are no nasty shocks at the end of the month

49. Get over your embarrassment and always ask for a discount wherever you shop. And be aware of any discounts you are entitled to at your place of work. Maybe your employer can get you discounts at particular shops, or give you cheaper insurance?

50. Be on top of what you can get with your bank card e.g. travel insurance if you pay for your airfare by credit card

51. Don't take money out of another bank's ATM as you will pay a couple of dollars for the luxury (okay, it's only small but it can buy you a coffee).

And one last thing...

52. Don't smoke (you know all the reasons why). If you can't give up, cut back.

CASE STUDY: GETTING YOUR BUDGET INTO THE BLACK

Louis did a first draft of his budget and to his horror found that he was spending $2300 more than he was earning each year. He knew this couldn't continue so he had a chat with his friends and thought hard about how he could earn more money and spend less.

He knew the next door neighbour's son was sports mad and the mother had an issue with childcare, so being a bit of a spin bowling legend himself, he offered to look after the son and play sport with him during term-time for a couple of hours a week. She was happy to pay him $30 each time, which gave him $960 a year. He set up an eBay account and started selling DVDs and books, getting about $30 a month ($360 a year), he began taking his lunch to work three days a week saving $30 a week, (or $1560 a year) and he made home-made pizzas every Sunday night instead of ordering take-away ($1040 a year).

He also finally learnt to use the coffee machine at work and twice a week made a coffee in the office rather than buying one (saving $400 a year). These five small changes meant that when he added up his extra earnings and savings, he was pleased to see that he'd added $4320 a year to the bottom line and was $2020 in the black. He could finally afford that holiday to Fiji.

Lesson: Small weekly changes can make a big difference to your budget

---

Shopping On-line

Shopping on-line is one of the joys of life but can be tricky (a bit like your love life). Here are a few tips to help you have smooth sailing:

• When you are shopping on line, use a secure payment method such as PayPal or BPay. It is not difficult to set up a PayPal account – all you need is an email address and a credit or debit card. Once set up, it means that when you buy something from a website, you only hand over your email address, and not your credit card details. Avoid making payments by transfers or direct debit

• Whenever you are making a payment, make sure that you look for the little padlock next to the URL and the letters HTTPS:// rather than just HTTP://. That little S makes all the difference – it means the site has SSL (Secure Sockets Layer) and that your payment is secure

• Use familiar websites and be critical of things that look odd. That spelling mistake or dodgy logo probably mean that it's a fake website

• Check that the company has a street address on the website

• Don't use free WiFi in public areas to do your banking or on-line shopping. It is not secure

• Check your statements to see that you've only bought what you wanted to buy

• Don't give out too much information. For instance, if you feel there is no need to provide your address but the website demands it, enter in 'Unwilling to divulge address' as the street name, and then your local CBD and CBD postcode. If you need to provide a phone number but you don't want to, enter 9000 0000. And if they want your birthday, enter 01/01 of your birth year

• Never answer emails asking for more information or start dealing with a seller by email – information should only be provided through a website

• Check that what you are buying will actually work in Australia

---

CASE STUDY: AN EXPENSIVE TOOTHBRUSH

Anni (yep, that's the author) and her dentist were discussing the merits of those high-pressure water flossers. He told her that people who use them have great dental hygiene and that she should consider buying one. A quick look on-line told her that they were half the price in the U.S. compared to Australia, so she quickly ordered one and congratulated herself on being so frugal. Being not quite so clever as she thought she was, it sadly took her more than a couple of days to remember that the voltage was different in the two countries and that the plug shape was not the same.

She assured herself that there would most likely be a switch on the side of the machine to change the voltage. There wasn't. She had to buy both an adaptor for the plug (cheap) and a voltage convertor (expensive) to make it work. It would have been better to stroll down the street and buy the machine locally.

Lesson: Think about whether that item from overseas will actually work

---

• Be careful about the cost of anything you are buying and don't forget about different currencies, postage, packaging and taxes

• Always check the terms and conditions of any transaction, and either print out a copy, save a .pdf or take a screen shot for your records

• If it looks too good to be true, it probably is. Check anything potentially dodgy at the Australian Competition and Consumer Commission (ACCC *Scamwatch* website[16]

• Make sure your anti-viral software is up to date

• And finally, at the end of the day, turn off your computer so potential hackers don't have unimpeded access.

Mobile Phone Contracts

Your dad gave you his old phone when you were in Year 10 – it's got a $15 monthly limit and the handset is appalling. Finally the contract's up and you can choose your own phone and plan – but sadly you're paying for it now. Here's what you should know.

Phone technologies

Australia has two technologies – GSM and 3G. GSM is good for basic features (calls, SMS) but 3G offers more features such as the ability to watch mobile TV (yeah, like you need more TV in your life) and the Internet.

Phone features

The more features you have on your phone, the more expensive it's going to be. Think about what's important to you and what you really need. Some plans come with a brand spanking new phone – do you really need it or can you beg, borrow or steal an alternative? Don't just roll over a contract because of the joy of getting a new phone if it's a crap contract. Do your research.

Plans

When you are considering a new phone plan, make sure you think about the total cost of each option, including the cost of the phone as well as access fees, usage charges and insurance. $0 upfront for a phone may be very enticing but could end up costing a whammy each month so discuss with your friends what plans they use and then check on-line and on comparison websites.

There are three types of plans to consider.

1. Pre-paid plans

You can choose to have a pre-paid plan, which is where you provide your own handset, pay a set amount each month, and then work your way through the credit throughout the month. If you spend over that limit, you will either be denied access, or revert to a pre-set cost per call, text or data download. This can be expensive. But while calls, texts and download are more expensive on pre-paid plans, generally these plans are good because they tend to keep you out of debt if you overuse.

2. Fixed contract

A fixed contract is usually for between 12-36 months, and may or may not include a handset. The phone will often be locked to the provider and there is a hefty fee if you try to end the contract early. You will need to decide which level of cap will suit you (say $49) and then you will get free calls and texts within this cap. The higher the cap, the cheaper the cost per call, text and download, and the more bonuses you get (such as free calls that don't count towards the cap).

Once you go over your limit you will need to pay a pre-set, usually substantial, charge for any further usage. If you find that you are going over your cap each month, it is usually cheaper to go onto a higher plan than to pay the extra usage charges.

3. Monthly contract

You can also get a monthly contract, which operates in a similar fashion to a fixed contract but which you can terminate at any time. These are generally offered by smaller suppliers – even supermarkets have phone plans (yeah, go figure!).

Coverage

Not all providers give mobile phone access to all geographical areas. On the provider's website you will be able to check whether your favourite places (e.g. a regular holiday destination) will be covered. Major urban centres are covered by all companies though you may find 'black spots' where coverage is poor.

Critical Information Summaries

Before making a decision, make sure you check out your plan's CIS (Critical Information Summary). All telcos have to provide one and it will give you information about what your phone will actually cost in simple language that you can easily compare. Every plan will have a CIS on the providers' website.

Checklist: Comparing phone plans

- Have you thought about whether you want to buy your phone independently, buy it as part of a package, or use one you have already?
- If you have reached the end of your contract, have you thought about going elsewhere rather than automatically getting a new phone and rolling over the contract?
- Do you know what sort of plan you will choose – pre-paid, fixed contract or monthly contract?
- How will you use your phone – are you the Queen of Texts, a midnight internet trawler, or do you like to make early morning calls? Find a plan that suits your usage
- Do you know if the plan charges per second or per 30-second block? Per second works out cheaper
- Are calls the same price at any time of day? Or, are they variable? Think about when you use your phone most
- Have you checked the coverage of the provider?
- Have you compared the CIS of each of the plans you are considering?
- If you are buying second-hand, have you checked the International Mobile Equipment Identity number (IMEI) on the Lost AMTA website to see if it's been stolen?
- And finally, have you talked with your friends about the plans they are using?

Keep your phone and yourself safe

- Make sure you regularly back up your phone to your computer. In particular, make sure you back up your photos, calendar and address book
- It's simple, but make sure you use the PIN to lock your phone
- Keep your phone safe in your bag or pocket and treat it as you would your wallet
- Make a note of your phone's IMEI (International Mobile Equipment Identity) by dialling *#06#. Keep it somewhere other than stored on your phone
- Make sure you enter a contact for use in an emergency under 'ICE' (in case of emergency) in your phone's address book and if possible, put your blood type in the notes section. If you are involved in an accident and are still conscious, it can save precious time
- Check your phone statement for unusual charges
- Be aware that 18 or 1800 numbers are free calls, but numbers beginning with 13 or 1300 are not and can be expensive particularly if you are calling from a mobile
- If you don't pay your phone bill it will affect your credit rating.

• And never, never, never use your mobile phone while you are driving. Don't even glance at it to check a text. In some states it's illegal to even touch it when the car is on, even if you are pulled over at the side of the road. Please say you'll never do it.

What do you do if your phone is stolen?

If your phone has been stolen make sure you report it to your provider as soon as possible. You are responsible for any costs incurred on your phone until you do so. (For further details, read *What to do if you lose your phone* on page 224).

What Do You Do If You Are Broke?

If you've got demand letters and final notices pouring through your letterbox, be brave and face the situation. You are not alone and do not need to be embarrassed. Most people have financial stress at some stage in their lives.

• Go and get advice from a free financial counsellor. If you are at uni, there will be one at Student Services, otherwise look on your local council's website for advice. Google 'financial help' and see what they have available
• Alternatively, get on to the Federal Government's Human Services website and look up 'Financial Information Service'[18]. This is free and confidential
• Check with your employer too, as many larger companies have a counsellor available for employees at no cost. Talk to them about what options are available to you. And don't worry – it will be confidential
• To give you some breathing space, ring your suppliers (e.g. for electricity, gas and phone) and tell them that you want to pay their bill but are not in a position to do so at the moment. Often they are happier to set up a gentle payment plan than to think you won't pay at all. And it will stop the scary letters
• For the short-term, can you sell something from around the house? An un-used piece of gym equipment? Your old text books or some DVDs? How about the bike or sewing-machine you never use?
• How about doing some part-time work around the neighbourhood? Offer to babysit for those family friends down the road, or do some gardening for your elderly neighbour
• Talk to your friends – they may know of a part-time job going where they work
• And while you're talking to them, ask your friends for the support that you need. I'm not talking about money here, just a shoulder to cry on or a nice cup of tea. It won't solve your financial situation but will make you feel much better.

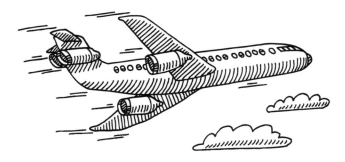

Travelling Overseas

You've slaved for months to earn enough moulah to get you away overseas, so the last thing you want is to be separated from your money on the way. There are a few things to remember.

Travel insurance on your credit card

Check it out with the bank first, but often if you pay for your air ticket on your credit card it will automatically give you travel insurance. This means that if you need to cancel because of illness, or you lose your baggage in Barcelona, you are covered. Just make sure that you have the cash ready to pay the credit card bill in the first month, otherwise you'll be paying interest from now till the cows (and you) come home.

Accessing cash

Don't take the currency of your destination with you – get it at the airport as you arrive via your ATM card. You will pay a small fee to your own bank (less than $10), but the withdrawal fee will be more than offset by the better exchange rate you'll get. Make sure you don't take out small amounts each time – take out a large-ish amount (say more than $100) and store most of it in your money belt. Don't do this if you are going to find the nearest pub and spend it all in one night. Der.

Don't be tempted to exchange money at the airport at a foreign exchange office – they will either have huge fees or a really poor rate – and sometimes both.

Another way to take your money is to take a travel card with you that is pre-loaded in the currency of your choice. Personally, I find this a hassle and you should be aware that large fees can be attached to their use. On the other hand though (and I like to be fair), these cards can be good if you plan to stay in dodgy places where the card might find its way into someone else's pocket. Those slimy thieves will then only be able to access the money on that card, not all the money in your account. If you choose to take a travel card, shop around for one with the best rates and fees.

Keeping it safe

If you are travelling with someone trustworthy, split your valuables. (And if they're not trustworthy, why are you travelling with them?) Give them a card of yours so if that if you lose your wallet, all is not lost. Use a money belt to keep most of your valuables in – the ones round your neck are great but can be annoying and rub in hot weather as well as being obvious; some people like the waist ones but if you are a girl (or a boy who likes wearing frocks), have you ever tried to access one in a dress? With a money belt storing most of your valuables, you can then use a wallet in your bag or pocket with just a small amount of everyday cash in it.

In terms of insurance, check out your normal contents insurance at home to see if it covers goods being taken overseas, such as your laptop or phone. You may be able to itemise them on your policy for as little as $4 a month to cover them while you are away. You can also sometimes insure your phone through your telecommunications provider but this can be expensive.

Which currency?

When you're away, only buy things in the local currency – anything you see in Australian or U.S. dollar prices will be overpriced. And always know the value of your currency...

CASE STUDY: LOCAL CURRENCY

Lucy is in Indonesia and is having a blast at the local market. She finds a groovy little dress for Rp100,000 or A$14 and decides to pay in dollars because it seems so cheap. Little does she know that the price in Rupiah is worth just over A$10, so she has just paid 40% more than she needed.

Lesson: Always know the value of the local currency, and pay in it

---

Keeping in touch

Be really, really careful using your phone overseas, particularly if your phone is from Australia. For some reason Australian telcos love to gouge you in any way they can while you are away and you can be presented with a truly horrible bill as a travel souvenir when you get home. If you are very disciplined and just want a phone to receive calls and texts, you can buy a worldwide SIM card at home before you go. If you want to have a full-service phone, better to buy a

SIM card when you arrive at your destination airport – depending on what you are after they can be as little as $20.

Alternatively you can also use email or local international phone calling cards to keep in contact with your family. Your mother will be going bananas if you don't contact her, so put her out of her misery. But do it cheaply.

CASE STUDY – KEEPING IN TOUCH

Two friends, Harriet and Sophie, go overseas together for a month. Harriet's boyfriend rings her every morning and night for a quick 2-minute call, and she sends him one text a day. She also downloads two 3-minute YouTube videos when she has had a few too many sangrias one night. Sophie emails her mates whenever there is free WiFi and buys an international calling card for $10 while she's away to make her calls.

While Sophie pays a total of $10 to keep in touch, Harriet is horrified that her bill is $442.50 when she gets home. She didn't realise that her provider charged her 75c every time she sent a text, $2 per minute to receive (yes, receive) a call and $3 per MB of data download.

Lesson: Don't use your home phone plan overseas

Give away those coins

Coins are useless outside their own country and can't be changed back at home, so either buy a drink or something cheap just before you leave, or put them in the UNICEF envelope on the plane on the way home. Lighten your wallet AND get good karma too!

Checklist: Getting good value when you travel

• Don't spend your precious money on water – if you're in a country where the water is potable (meaning able to be drunk, not able to be put in a pot!), make sure you always ask for tap water rather than buying the bottled stuff. You'll save heaps

• Don't eat or drink at places that have big signs in English. You can bet that these are tourist traps and will cost you big time. Enjoy picnics with food from supermarkets or local stores

• Eat up big at that breakfast buffet. In theory it might stop you having to buy lunch (although it doesn't work for me)

• Unless it's for safety reasons, use the public transport system. It's the way the locals go so you'll see more of local life than if you are stuck in a taxi

• Travel in the off-season: in Europe and the U.S. this will mean travelling outside June to September and in Asia, it means travelling in the rainy or hot seasons. This makes it much cheaper but there are reasons they are the off-season – usually climatic!

• Do your research before you go, both on the 'net and by taking guide books with you. Don't spend a fortune on your travel and then be stingy with your travel guide book – just one or two really good tips can save you the cost of the book

• Look at booking some things before you leave – for instance, booking a trip up the Eifel Tower can save you 4 hours in a queue – and who wants to spend a precious day in Paris in a line?

Five Top Tips

1. Practice good money habits. Frugal is the new black. Try to earn as much as possible, spend as little as possible and save the difference. It's the recipe for financial happiness!

2. When you are shopping on-line, use a secure payment method such as PayPal or BPay. Don't hand over your card details to just anyone on-line and be on the lookout for dodgy websites. Think poor grammar, spelling mistakes, blurry logos and requests for too much information

3. If your phone gets stolen, report it immediately. You are responsible for any calls, texts or data downloads on it until you do

4. If you are broke, seek help early. Take a deep breath and take action before it gets out of control

5. If you travel overseas, buy a SIM card at your destination to make calls and send texts. You'll be slugged if you don't.

FINDING THAT PERFECT JOB

So you've moved out and things are looking a little grim on the money front. You're not much of a card shark and you're too clumsy to be a cat burglar. Looks like you'll have to get a job. Bugger.

Short On Time? Read This.

1. Use your networks. If you haven't worked before you might think you don't have any, but think of your school friends, parents' friends, sports friends, people at the gym or the park and your neighbours. Get out there and talk to everyone – people like to help

2. You need a good CV as a starting point when you are looking for a job. There's not just one perfect format so take advice, get on-line and spend some time developing a good one

3. Become familiar with and practice the STAR (Situation, Task, Action, Result) technique for answering questions in competency-based interviews. This gives you a framework to answer questions when the interviewers ask you to describe a situation where you displayed one of the skills they're looking for

4. Prepare yourself for your interview. Think of questions you're likely to be asked and work out your answers in advance, do some research, get in some practice and be as friendly and relaxed as you can be

5. Be careful how your on-line presence portrays you as a potential employee. When the interviewer asks you to show them your Facebook page, are you going to be happy with what they see? More importantly, are they?

What Type Of Job Are You After?

If this is your first time in the workforce, you might be looking for something part-time that will fit in with your uni course. This could involve babysitting, flipping burgers, or just holiday work between semesters. Generally you will need to start pounding the pavement, dropping in on likely businesses with your CV (Curriculum Vitae) in hand. A smile on your dial will go a long way. It can be really hard without experience, but everyone was in the same boat once and you'll get there. Keep at it.

Alternatively, you may now be looking for that first full-time job. This is really daunting territory as there's so much more at stake. You could be in this job for several years, and while changing jobs can be a fact of life with part-time work, it's not so acceptable for permanent jobs. This chapter will help you in your search.

Where To Look

Use networks

Everyone has networks that can be useful in looking for a job. Perhaps you play tennis with someone who is working in an interesting company, or your mum's best friend is in the same line of work you'd like to be in. Is there a teacher from your old school or a tutor at uni that you really clicked with and who might be able to help? Maybe your friend's employer is looking for an extra hand, or how about the people you've met when you've done work experience or volunteering? Make sure that you talk to everyone about what it is you're looking for and ask for their assistance if you think they might be able to help. Don't be worried that you are using people – generally people are happy to help.

Your aim in using your networks is to get a foot in the door and to differentiate yourself from everyone else who is applying for the same job. Perhaps you'll get the chance to meet with the Head of Human Resources, or get the name of someone you can talk with. After that it will be up to you, but often the first step is the hardest.

Research

One way to get a job is to directly approach companies you are interested in. Start by doing some research in your industry. Who would you like to work for? Draw up a potential list of target companies, find out a bit more about them and then ring them (see *How to Cold Call A Company* just coming up in this chapter on page 69).

Where do you find a job?

Twenty years ago every advertised job was listed in the local newspapers. It was a simple matter to get the Saturday papers and a big red texta, and to circle the ones that appealed. These days, you'll find that while newspapers have days dedicated to certain industries, the bulk of jobs aren't in the newspaper at all. You might be lucky and find one, but you'd do better to look on-line.

Your first stop should be to get onto a business networking website such as Linkedin[19]. Here you can upload your CV, look for jobs that might be of interest, research industries and companies, join discussion groups and further build your network. Even more importantly though is the fact that employers can find you.

You should also look at job websites such as Jobs, Seek or CareerOne[20]. While each site is slightly different, you can generally search for available jobs using key words, salary levels, location and industry. You can also set up alerts so you are automatically notified when a suitable job is listed, and when you find one, you can apply via the website.

Volunteering and work experience

Sometimes you have the opportunity to volunteer or do work experience at a company you might be interested in. This gives you a chance to get to know the organisation a bit better and to get some experience, but it also gives them a risk-free way of getting to see you in action. Play your cards right and have a bit of luck on your side, and they may end up taking you on permanently.

How To Cold Call A Company

Cold calling a company is enough to make anyone's blood run cold. It's awful but here's a way to do it with the least angst possible:

- Identify the company you want to approach
- Ring and ask to speak to the HR (Human Resources) department. If possible, get the name of someone in that department from reception
- Introduce yourself by name and say that you are interested in finding employment
- Say what sort of job you're after, what your skills and experience are and why you like their company. Be brief – people are busy
- Ask if you can please send in a CV and who should you address it to
- Thank them for their time.

There, was that so bad?

How To Create A Written Application

A written application for a job consists of a cover letter and an accompanying CV. Sometimes 'CV' can be used interchangeably with the word 'Resumé' but the latter is generally shorter and less-detailed.

You should put together a master CV including all your skills, experience and qualifications, then tailor it for each job application. This is in no way suggesting that you tell a few porkies (you're not that sort of person, are you?), but just that you include experience and information that is relevant or appropriate for the job at hand. Never, ever lie on a CV about your skills or experience, or be boastful or unrealistic about what you can achieve for the company. It is worth noting here that there are enormous amounts of websites devoted to writing CVs, and many will have samples of CVs and accompanying letters, so have a look till you find a style that suits you. Don't plagiarise (no! no! no!) but make use of the ideas you find. Alternatively, have a look below.

General formatting and layout

- Use a spell checker and a grammar checker as any typos or spelling mistakes are deadly. Get a literate friend to check over your CV for you
- Did you miss that? Make sure that you get someone else to read your CV and correct any mistakes you might have made. Nothing will turn off a potential employer faster than a stupid mistake – it makes you look sloppy or worse, not very bright
- Use plain professional English with no abbreviations unless they are so common that anyone reading them will understand them
- Use standard white A4 copying paper; 80gsm is fine. You should use a simple font such as Times New Roman, 12 point. Now is not the time to use coloured paper or the Zapf Dingbats font to express your inner quirkiness – it will just make you stand out (but in a really bad way)
- Include a footer with your name and email address on every page
- Leave large margins and lots of white space. It looks much more controlled and aesthetically pleasing. If there is little white space it can look like you've rushed your CV, or that you are so desperate you are including everything
- Use bold for headings, and dot points throughout for clarity
- If sending your CV by email, either send it as an attachment or as a .pdf to make sure that the formatting doesn't get mucked up.

Cover letter

- This should be written on one side of the page on white A4 copy paper
- Write a new letter for each job application – it can be easy to spot a 'one size fits all' letter
- Address the letter to a specific person and keep it formal e.g. address it

to 'Mr Jones' and not to 'Andrew' or 'to whom it may concern'
- Say why you are interested in the job and the industry
- Make sure your letter explains why you think you would be suitable for the position and what you can bring to the organisation
- Make sure you pick up a few key words from the ad and include them (but try not to be too obvious!).

Curriculum Vitae

- Don't make it too long – two or three A4 pages are fine, and only one page if it's for a part-time job.
- Leave out anything from your master CV that is not relevant to the job for which you are applying
- Make sure that points you wish to highlight are easy to see and if there is more than one page that they fall on the first page. This will make them more evident to the interviewer who may well be sifting through piles and piles of CVs and wishing they were on a desert isle
- Remember, the heading should be your name and not 'Curriculum Vitae'.

Sample Layout For Your Curriculum Vitae

There are hundreds of ways to present your CV, and yours will be slightly different from your friend's, which in turn won't be the same as your dad's. Don't stress – get on-line and do a bit of research, or use the following as a guide. Concentrate on making it professional, clear and factual. The aim is to make you seem so appealing that they will want to employ you on the spot.

Contact details

- First name and family name as heading (don't worry about your middle name)
- Address
- Email address
- Mobile phone number
- There is no need to include your date of birth or marital status.

Key skills

- Write a list of your key skills including personal and business skills, computer skills and languages. Make sure you include those that are mentioned in the ad if you have them.

Tertiary education

- Work in reverse order, so last comes first
- List the date of completion, the name of the course and the institution you attended

- Include any relevant details that relate to the position, including scholarships and awards.

Secondary education

- This section should be shorter than the section on tertiary education
- List the details of your final year at school and your ATAR or final score
- Also list any major achievements, awards or leadership positions and any overseas study.

Employment history

- Again, in reverse date order, list your employment history including your starting and ending dates, the job title, the name of the organisation and dot points of your key responsibilities
- Don't automatically disregard any part-time jobs you have held – there may be skills that you have developed that are transferable.

Professional memberships

- List the period of your membership, the level of membership and the organisation's name.

Professional training or further development

- In reverse-date order, list the name of any training courses you have completed, the length of the course and the provider.

Voluntary work

- List any volunteer work you have completed including dates, your role and the name of the organisation with dot points of key responsibilities
- You could include work with church groups, sporting organisations, organisations for the elderly, life-saving duty etc.

Extra-curricular activities and hobbies

- List your hobbies and extra-curricular activities. Don't include too much detail but try to think about what might be relevant or appropriate for the job at hand.

Referees

- Make sure that your referees are happy to support you in the job application and ask them before you mention them in your CV. Never include someone's name if you haven't yet asked, even if you are 100% sure that they would be happy to support you
- List the name, title and contact details of your referees, but do not

include the references themselves
- Don't go overboard, make them relevant, and do what the employer asks: if they want two referees, give them two, not seven
- And don't forget to thank your referees.

Advice About Interviews

So you've got an interview! Well done! Whether the interview will be by phone or in person, you need to make some preparations beforehand.

Prepare yourself

Get on to the organisation's website and do a bit of research about the company and if you can, your particular division or area of work. Think about what's required in the job and what skills or competencies you might need to do the job well. These are often listed in the ad.

This preparation can be extremely useful when you come across a competency-based interview. This means that instead of a free-flowing chat, the interviewers will be using the time to establish whether or not you have the required skills for the job. You may be asked about a situation that has arisen in the past and how you handled it. So, before you have the interview, you need to put together examples of how you have previously demonstrated the required competencies, and a very good way of doing this is to use the STAR technique: Situation, Task, Action and Result.

CASE STUDY: USING THE STAR TECHNIQUE

Zara was being interviewed for a job as a Programme Leader at the local university. She had thought hard about examples from her previous work life and how they related to the competencies required so when the interviewer asked her to talk about a time she had to problem solve under pressure, Zara was able to answer fluently.

"I was working as a Programme Leader in the Diploma of Economics course, and late in the afternoon I got a call saying that Jack, the lecturer for the Macroeconomics class that evening, was unwell and couldn't attend (Situation).

"I had to quickly find a replacement so that the students hadn't all travelled into the city after work, only to find that the lecturer was absent (Task).

"I consulted the list of Macroeconomics lecturers to find one and discovered that Annabelle was not scheduled to work that night, so I contacted her to see if she was available. She was. I then organised for Jack to email his lecture plan and notes to her. (Action).

"When the students arrived, Annabelle explained the situation to them and covered for Jack, and the students were happy to have their lecture as normal (Result).

Lesson: Prepare to use the STAR technique to answer competency-based questions

So, make sure you look at what competencies will be required in your position, and ahead of time think of examples from your previous work life (or personal life if this is your first job) which can be answered using the STAR technique. Don't make it obvious to the interviewer that you are answering using this method – the aim is to make them think that you are just providing a coherent answer to the question. Be brief to keep the interviewer's interest, and be specific, using names, so that it is more realistic. And don't fib!

Think of other questions you might be asked and practice answers to them. For example, they might ask you how your skills might suit you to the job or how your previous experience might be relevant. Don't forget the old chestnuts 'what are your strengths and weaknesses?' and 'where do you see yourself in five years' time?'

And finally, think of some questions that you can ask. These could be about career paths or company structure, or you could throw in one that will indicate you've done your homework e.g. "how do you see the recent changes in the parent company affecting the role of the organisation here?" Don't ask about money. Be prepared to discuss it if they raise it; otherwise save it for a later stage of the recruitment process.

Practice makes perfect

If you can, take advantage of the careers office at a university as some offer one-on-one interview practice; otherwise practice with a supportive friend. If all else fails, try the dog. (I personally find that dogs are quite non-judgemental.)

Some people swear by standing in front of the mirror and practicing although I usually feel like a goose and end up being distracted. Why's my hair standing up like that? What's that strange shadow on my face? But have a go – if it works for you, that's great.

And during the interview

Be prepared to sell yourself. This is one time when it won't work in your best interests to be modest, but never lie about what you have done or will be able to do for the company. Frame your weaknesses in a positive light e.g. "one weakness I have is that I tend to be a perfectionist", but don't be too obvious.

Don't speak too quickly and don't mumble. If they ask you to repeat yourself it doesn't necessarily mean they are reacting to something you've said in a negative way – maybe it's just that their years of hanging out in clubs mean their hearing's shot.

And finally, try to keep your nerves under control. It might be important but it's not the only company in the world, and certainly not the only job. What's the worst that can happen? Maybe you'll vomit on the interview desk or drop the 'F' bomb five times by mistake. So what? It'll make a great story later on!

Phone Interviews

If you have sent in your CV, you may be asked for a phone interview.

Checklist: Phone interview

- Go to the bathroom beforehand and have a drink of water handy, but no food! It'll just sound weird if you are crunching throughout the phone call
- Have some tissues available in case. No, not because you'll be crying! You might need to (surreptitiously) blow your nose
- Do you need any papers? Are there documents that might be useful?
- Have a pen and paper to write down questions or make notes
- Make sure that you have turned off your mobile phone (unless they are ringing you on it – der), put the dog outside and shut yourself in a quiet room

- Make yourself feel professional – don't do the interview in your underwear!
- Phone interviews are tricky as there are no non-verbal cues, so it's even more important than normal to sound interested and friendly. Try to remember the name of the interviewer and don't get distracted – hey, what was that out the window?
- At the end of the interview, thank them then the following day shoot them off a thank-you email, re-expressing your interest in the job and that you are looking forward to hearing from them.

Interviews In Person

Or maybe you've got an interview in person.

Checklist: Personal interview

- Before the big day, ring and ask about the format of the interview and ask if there is anything else that you can send in that would be useful to the interviewers. This shows you are keen and have initiative
- Don't be late! Plan ahead and aim to be early even if you're absolutely sure how long it will take to get there
- Dress appropriately, and of course make sure your clothes are clean and well-ironed. Make sure your shoes are in a good state of health, too
- Turn off your phone. Yep, off
- Be friendly and confident, even if you don't feel it. And of course, be polite
- At the end, ask what the process is from here on in, and thank them for their time
- Again, shoot them off a thank-you email, re-expressing your interest in the job and that you are looking forward to hearing from them
- You can follow up with a phone call if you don't hear from them in the next week or so.

And one final thought

It is not unheard of for employers to check what you've been doing on-line and they will make judgements about you from what they find. So think about how you want to be perceived and if necessary delete those postings that might form the wrong impression.

(And by the way, if you have zero on-line presence, you will be well sought after for a job as a spy.)

Good luck!

Five Top Tips

1. Make sure your CV is perfect in terms of grammar, spelling and typos. Get your smartest friend to check it out, or even your parents

2. Write a new cover letter for each application. It's easy to spot one that is generic and it's insulting to the interviewer to think you can't be bothered writing a new one

3. Be prepared to sell yourself in an interview. It might feel weird telling strangers how wonderful you are but now is not the time to be self-effacing

4. But that doesn't mean lying or exaggerating. We want the truth, the whole truth and nothing but the truth – but it can be sugar-coated. And the whole truth might be a bit too revealing actually...

5. And a no-brainer – don't be late for your interview! Plan to arrive half an hour early and spend the time quietly practicing and calming yourself.

CHAPTER **5**

KITCHEN ESSENTIALS

We've all got a bit of Heston Blumenthal in us but most likely this is the first time you have had your own kitchen and managed your own food budget. Do you feel excited? Or maybe terrified? Don't worry – I'm here to help.

Haven't Got Time To Read The Whole Chapter? Read This.

1. If both your larder and your wallet are empty, go visit a 'pay as much as you can' restaurant. Or look to see where you can volunteer and then be fed. Think churches, missions and soup kitchens

2. Make food presents for your friends and family. A home-made cake on a birthday can be more meaningful than an expensive gift, and jams and chutneys last forever and are always welcome

3. Raw meat can have lots of bacteria so keep it away from cooked foods. Make sure you wash the plate that your uncooked steak was on before you put the cooked version back. Clean up meaty spills on your bench, and store raw meat on the bottom shelf of your refrigerator to avoid it dripping on other food

4. Don't buy takeaway

5. Did you miss that? Don't buy takeaway. It's expensive and bad for you. Make it a big treat for special occasions and not a weekly occurrence.

Basic Kitchen Equipment

You've probably come from a kitchen that has been really well-equipped and if you've cooked before, you're used to having whatever you need at hand. It's unrealistic to expect that your own kitchen will be that well-kitted out at the start, but here's a list of essentials you can work towards owning.

You can get most of these items second-hand at Vinnies, but you'll find that over time friends and family will come up with bits and pieces they don't need and which they're happy to pass on to you. You certainly don't need to rush out and buy everything on the list on the first day out of home.

Checklist: Kitchen equipment

- A couple of non-stick saucepans, say one large and one small, and with glass lids if you can. Glass lids make all the difference – you can check what's going on in there without opening the lid and losing all that heat. They absolutely must be non-stick – life's too short to be scrubbing saucepans! If you are concerned about the safety of non-stick saucepans, never fear and check out the *Low Fat Cooking* website[21]
- At least one non-stick frying pan – if it has reasonable sides and can double as a wok, so much the better
- Something to stir with – I would suggest two wooden spoons of different sizes
- A chopping board – wooden is best to keep your knives sharp
- Something to scrape with – a silicon spatula is good
- A large mixing bowl. If you need a small one use a cereal bowl
- A colander (also known as a drainer or 'that thing with holes in it')
- A slotted spoon (a big spoon with holes for draining say peas out of the saucepan – also known as 'that other thing with holes in it')
- A pair of tongs – supermarket ones are perfect
- A wide flat spatula with long holes in it (technically called a fish slice though I've never used mine for fish)
- A baking tray to fit your oven. New ovens come with their own, but at a rental property they have often disappeared

- A 20cm/8" silicon round cake tin (these are unsteady so sit it on your baking tray to cook). An aluminium one is fine too but can be a drag as you'll need to line it with baking paper each time you use it
- A 12 hole silicon muffin tray (again, sit it on a tray to cook)
- A pie dish – good for savoury or dessert pies or puddings
- A small hand-held mixer. It will make life a lot easier although a wooden spoon and lots of effort can give the same result
- If you're into soups, a blender – stick or otherwise
- A cooling rack
- A sifter or a fine sieve
- A vegie peeler
- A grater
- A garlic crusher
- A round cutter for scones or biscuits
- Measuring cups (1 cup, ½ cup, ¼ cup, ⅓ cup) or a measuring jug with the same measurements
- Measuring spoons (1 tablespoon, 1 teaspoon, ½ teaspoon, ¼ teaspoon)
- Baking paper, aluminium foil, cling wrap
- A pastry brush
- This book, of course. Also an Internet connection so you can look up recipes. Try the *Taste* website – if you can't find what you're looking for, it doesn't exist. Well, almost.

Food Budgeting

You're going to realise pretty quickly once you move out of home that one, the fridge doesn't refill itself (damn!), and two, food is really expensive. You'll need to stick to a budget or else food shopping will eat up all your available cash. Try these tips to get more bang for your buck:

1. Write a list and don't shop when you're hungry – you'll buy more

2. Check your fridge before you write your shopping list, and try to plan meals so that you use up everything you have. Be creative and don't let food go off. There are websites that can help you. One that is fun to use is *Big Oven*[23] – just enter three ingredients you have in your fridge and it will give you recipes. Sweet

3. Shop at the supermarket. I can guarantee you that people will tell you to go to the market for the best produce. That's great if you enjoy hanging out there, having coffee, meeting friends, and whiling away a lazy Saturday morning. It's also great if you can happen to be there at the end of the day when they are heavily discounting excess produce. But if you're just after good food, then try your local supermarket. They have such massive turnover you're pretty sure of getting fresh produce there and if you find you have a problem with something, you can always take it back for a refund, no questions asked

4. Only take the amount of cash with you that you have allocated for supermarket shopping and leave your cards at home

5. Okay – this is going to appear obvious but buy food when it's on sale and when it's in season. For example, don't buy your strawberries in winter; they're either hot-housed or have come from a looooooooong way away and that makes them expensive

6. Look at buying supermarket home brands. You'll need to work out over time which ones are okay, but you will be pretty safe with all your basic ingredients such as flour, sugar, milk etc.

7. Buy non-perishables such as toilet paper, washing powder and tinned tomatoes in bulk if you can afford to and have the storage space

8. Get to know the prices of things you often buy so you can tell where they are the cheapest

9. Make use of discount food stores such as NQR (Not Quite Right) – they have cheap food because it is near its use-by date or the packaging has been damaged

10. Don't buy takeaway. Don't buy takeaway. Repeat after me. Don't buy takeaway. It's expensive and it's unhealthy. Okay, it's great for a treat but you can cook up a meal quicker than you can organise a delivery – how about an omelette, some spaghetti carbonara or a big bowl of soup? Less than 20 minutes and you're done

11. Limit alcohol. Yep, lots of reasons to do it and one of them is cost

12. Go vegetarian, or at least try it a couple of times a week. In terms of cost of protein, meat's right up there. Try eggs or lentils. And speaking of lentils, even if you're having a meat meal, if it happens to be made of mince chuck in a handful. They're healthy, bulk the meal out and are cheap

13. Your freezer is your friend – did you know you can freeze bread and cakes perfectly? Just make sure they are well sealed in plastic or they can get that white burnt texture of freezer burn. In the case of bread, you don't even need to defrost it, just pop it in the toaster. You can also freeze cream, milk, butter and citrus fruit for use in cooking at a later date

14. Meat is also good to freeze. Buy it on special and freeze it, particularly cheaper cuts which survive the cold environment brilliantly. But don't keep frozen meat longer than 6-12 months (and mince for only 3 months)

15. Don't buy water in bottles. It's a total waste of money and all those bottles have to end up somewhere. Here's a horrible statistic – 60 million bottles A DAY (yep, you read that right) are thrown away in the U.S. and the water in those bottles costs up to 4,000 times more than the water out of the tap[24].

16. Make food presents to give to people. You could make jam and chutney (see Chapter 6 of this book), or how about a home-made birthday cake? It is certainly more meaningful than anything you could pick up at a shop

17. Have a green thumb? Try to grow vegies in whatever space you have available outside. You can start small with herbs or try tomatoes, which are easy to grow in a pot, then move on to other vegies. Speak to your neighbours to find out what works for them as they have the same soil and climate as you.

Essential Food Items To Keep On Hand

Sometimes you just don't have the money or the time to go shopping so it's good to know that you can make a meal out of what's already in your cupboard. Here is a list of food items you should always have on hand and which will allow you to cook a decent meal. These are all cheap and, apart from the eggs and butter, you should stock up on them when you see them on sale. Unlike the kitchen equipment, if you can afford them, I'd buy them all on day one of living away from home.

From the list below you can make fried rice, tuna pasta, omelettes, vegie curry, porridge, eggs on toast, butter cake, tuna stir fry, pasta with corn sauce, plain biscuits, French toast, scones, risotto, sandwiches...the list goes on...

Checklist: Basics to have on hand

- Flour (both Self Raising and plain)
- Sugar
- Eggs
- Butter
- Oil
- Rice
- Oats
- Pasta
- Bread (store in the freezer)
- Frozen peas
- Tinned tuna
- Tinned tomatoes
- Tinned corn
- Curry powder or paste
- Soy sauce
- Stock cubes
- UHT milk

Food Storage

Cupboards

If you can, store all open packets of dry goods in containers in your cupboards to avoid moths. Moths are sneaky little buggers lying dormant in packets of food and ready to spring to life at the first chance so they can contaminate other food in your pantry. You know you have a moth problem if you see your food clumping together weirdly with wispy bits of what looks like spider web clinging to the edges of the container. I'm pretty sure moths don't have teeth but you wouldn't believe it as they can eat through plastic bags. Ugh. Common wisdom says that bay leaves can deter moths but I've never found this advice to be very helpful.

There's nothing much worse than moths in your pantry, apart from rats and mice. Clean up any spills or drips immediately, and make sure you wipe over the shelves in your pantry every now and then to keep rodents at bay. Borrowing a cat is a good non-toxic (at least for you) way of keeping rats and mice away.

Putting food in containers and wiping benches will also help keep ants away. If you do end up with an ant problem, there are ant-killing liquids you dot around the place and which are very effective. Personally, I'd rather rely on keeping things clean or even just put up with the ants than have these chemicals near food but lots of people swear by them.

Store wine in a dry area with an even temperature and don't move it around too much. Yep, a cellar is perfect but so is a cupboard. If the wine has real corks, store it on its side.

Fridge

Notice that the first place you visit when you go back to your parents' place is the fridge? That's because everyone knows the fridge can be the source of all joy!

You need to remember a few things to keep you and your food healthy. Store meat on the lowest shelf in the refrigerator so any drips can't fall onto food stored on a shelf below. This is to avoid cross-contamination of other foods with bacteria from the raw meat. Similarly, don't ever put cooked meat back on a plate which has held raw meat – wash it in between.

Remember that meat (particularly chicken) and seafood, eggs and dairy products pose the greatest risk in terms of food poisoning. You need to store these in the fridge and not leave them sitting out on the bench. So that means you shouldn't defrost food on the sink – plan ahead a bit and do it on a plate in the fridge, or in the microwave.

If you can, store foods in the fridge in glass or ceramic containers. You can use cling wrap over the top but try to avoid it touching the food. There is some concern about chemicals leaching from plastic into food, particularly if the food is hot, acidic, fatty or salty25.

And don't forget to wipe out your fridge every now and then with hot soapy water. You can add some vanilla to the water to make your fridge smell sweet. If something spills, wipe it up quickly – it's amazing how difficult things can be to get off the walls or shelves of the fridge once they're set.

What To Do With Leftovers

When you don't have lots of cash to splash, make sure you use up any leftovers in your fridge. Apart from making sense economically it can stretch your boundaries in terms of creativity. I remember a memorable *Apple Couscous Crumble* I made when there wasn't much in the pantry – unusual but delicious!

Checklist: What to do with leftovers

- Stale bread can be chopped up into dice, sprayed with oil and cooked in the oven to make croutons for soup
- Bread can also be dipped in beaten egg and vanilla, and fried in butter to make delicious French Toast
- Sour cream can be used to make scones instead of fresh cream
- Make black bananas into banana bread
- Chuck the hard rind of parmesan cheese into a stew or soup – it will give a lovely Parmesan-y flavour (go figure) to the soup
- Left-over meat makes a great curry– cut it all up, fry with some curry paste and add coconut milk to make a feast fit for a king. Or heat it up in the microwave in some gravy

- Cakes or biscuits can be crumbled on top of tinned or fresh fruit, then cooked in the oven to make a crumble. Or cut the cake up, and layer it with custard and jelly adding a good splash of sherry every now and then to make a trifle
- Old, hard cheese is fine in cheese sauce
- Left-over vegies make excellent soup. Just boil them in stock and puree
- Put left over vegies in quiche – any type will do!
- Top left-over anything (chicken, vegies, meat, the dog) with cheese sauce and place a piece of pre-rolled pasty cut to size on top, or use crumbled stale bread. Bake in a hot oven till golden brown for a delicious pie.

Emergency Eating

You've spent all your money again and now you're home and hungry and there's nothing to eat. What can you do?

- Go to a restaurant where you only pay as much as you can afford. For example, there's Lentil as Anything in both Sydney and Melbourne or Annalakshmi in Perth. Don't give much money this time but for good karma make sure you go back and give some to the owner when you have a bit more cash
- Find a soup kitchen – you might feel embarrassed, but everyone has a time when they need a helping hand. Google 'soup kitchen' and your city
- Do some volunteer work – apart from being good for your soul you will often get fed. And how great will you feel?
- Whatever you feel about religion, go to church – there are often refreshments after the services and they may be able to point you in the right direction for other cheap food options. Some churches run food programmes themselves, and you could either use the services offered, or offer to help out and you'll be sure to get a feed
- Keep an eye out in the local paper and find a focus group. It won't help you today but you will find that in exchange for your opinions, you are usually fed as well as being paid
- Attend free events (such as lectures or concerts) that include refreshments. There are lots around – you just need to track them down
- Go to your local food market at closing time to pick up some bargains – the vendors don't really want to have to pack up their perishable food to take home
- Barter with your friends and neighbours – perhaps you could swap your lemons for some eggs?
- Ask at some restaurants if they might be throwing out any food at the end of the night. Be polite if they refuse
- Also try bakeries at the end of the day – they are often happy to get rid of old bread as they can't easily sell it the next day

- If you are really desperate, go 'dumpster diving' at your local supermarket. They won't be happy if they find you going through their bins but there will be food just out of date that is perfectly good, as well as slightly over-ripe fruit and vegies. Lay low and try not to get caught
- And finally, visit members of your family! (Okay, maybe a last resort but along with an earful about how you need to plan better you'll get a free feed).

CASE STUDY: RUNNING OUT OF MONEY FOR FOOD

Hugh was down to his last $10 and his salary wouldn't hit his account till Friday afternoon. It was Tuesday morning. He had some cereal and milk so breakfasts were sorted and he could survive on cup noodles for other meals but things were still looking pretty grim. He remembered seeing a mission round the corner from work and thought he'd have a look at the website. He found they provided lunches for homeless people on Tuesdays and an evening support group for foreign students on Thursdays. Better still they were looking for volunteers.

He went along at lunchtime and had a chat with some very interesting people who had fallen on hard times as well as a huge feed. He was amazed at how good he felt afterwards. Then on Thursday after work he went to help out again for an hour and had a feast as well as practicing his Indonesian. All in all they were great experiences and he vowed to return, even when his finances were more under control.

And finally on Friday lunchtime he saw a notice saying that there was a lecture at work on the new accounting system, and lunch was provided. It sounded boring but he thought it was a fair trade-off and went along. At least the sandwiches were good.

Lesson: Look around for places where you can get fed for free

Five Top Tips

1. Immediately wipe up any spills in the stove, pantry or fridge – they're so much harder to clean up once they set and are even worse if they are cooked on

2. Shop at the supermarket. It's not very chic but their turnover is high and their prices are low, so you can be pretty sure of getting reasonable produce at a reasonable price. And if not, they will take it back

3. For better taste, nutrition and cost, buy food when it's in season and preferably grown locally. And buy things on special if you can store them and know you'll use them

4. To minimise the chance of food poisoning, don't mix raw and cooked foods and keep chicken, seafood, egg dishes and dairy well chilled. Don't leave them out on the bench

5. Shop when you have just eaten, keeping to a list and spending cash instead of using cards. All these things will help keep your budget under control.

CHAPTER 6

WHAT'S FOR DINNER?

t's 6:30pm. You've just walked in the door from work and you quickly realise there's no mum cooking dinner for you. Unless you're a serious fan of Weet-Bix and Milo, or have the budget and waistline that can cope with take-away every night, here are a few recipes that will happily keep body and soul together.

Haven't Got Time To Read The Whole Chapter? Read This.

1. If you're starving and want to eat as soon as possible, cook an omelette (5 minutes), a stir fry (10 minutes), risotto (15 minutes) or some soup (20 minutes). All faster than getting in your car and getting take away

2. Nothing in the fridge but a few old vegies? Make soup! You can put almost anything in with some stock (as long as it's edible), cook it up and it will taste fine

3. You can make a quick lasagne with just left-over bolognaise sauce, grated cheese and lasagne sheets. Alternate the layers, whack it in the oven and you're done

4. To test if a cake is done, gently touch the top with your finger – it should bounce back and feel dry if the cake is ready to come out of the oven. Check by inserting a skewer into the middle of the cake and if it comes out clean, the cake is ready

5. Jams and chutneys are not as tricky as you might think. They take a little bit of time but once you get the hang of them are economical and highly impressive as gifts.

Soup Recipes

Soup is great – it can be very healthy, it's cheap, you can use whatever you have in the fridge and it's really quick and easy to make. Oh, and it's delicious too! If you're not a soupy-type person, have a go. You never know, you might be converted.

Basic vegie soup

Ingredients

About 3 cups of chopped vegetables, whatever you feel like or is in season
1 onion, chopped
Butter or oil spray
Stock, or a stock cube + water
Bacon, chopped (optional)
Herbs, washed and chopped (optional)
Pepper and salt

Method

In a saucepan heat up the butter and oil together and fry the vegetables, onion, bacon and herbs if using for around 10 minutes. Add stock (or use a stock cube and water, 1 cube for every 1 cup of water) to cover the vegies and simmer (gently boil) for another 15 minutes or until the vegies are soft. Puree if you like. Add pepper and salt.

Some other good combinations include:

Cauliflower soup

Cook up the stalk and florets of cauliflower, a chopped onion and a few good shakes of curry powder in butter or oil as above, then add chicken stock to cover. Simmer as above. Puree.

Zucchini and bacon soup

Fry up a few rashers of bacon, chopped, then add chopped zucchini and fry as above. Add stock, simmer and puree.

Broccoli (and blue cheese) soup

Fry up the stalk and florets of broccoli, then cover with chicken stock and simmer as above. Once ready, add some blue cheese if you wish and puree.

Pumpkin soup

Fry up peeled and chopped pumpkin with a teaspoon each of cumin and ginger powder as above, then cover with stock. Simmer, then puree.

Lentil soup

Cook up onion, add a tin of tomatoes and ¾ cup uncooked lentils. Add beef stock to cover, simmer for 15 minutes or until lentils are soft.

Best ever roast vegie soup

Boil up left over roast vegies (carrot, sweet potato, potato, pumpkin, onion) in stock till soft, then puree. Magnificent!

Sauce Recipes

Sauces can be brilliant to dress up a simple meal – pour a mushroom sauce over steak or pasta, or how about a cheese sauce over macaroni? Start with a Béchamel (white sauce) and move on from there.

White sauce (Béchamel)

Ingredients

60g/2oz butter
⅓ cup plain flour
1 litre/4 cups milk
Pepper and salt
A pinch of nutmeg

Method

Melt the butter in a saucepan over a medium heat, then add the flour and stir to make a thick paste. Continue to cook this for two minutes, stirring all the time, until it is bubbling, then take it off the heat. Pour in the milk, little by little, whisking all the while. Once it's all incorporated and smooth, put it back on the heat and bring to the boil, stirring. The sauce is ready once it coats the back of spoon.

Cheese sauce

Take your white sauce off the heat and add a good handful of grated Parmesan or tasty cheese (or live on the wild side and add both) and half a teaspoon of prepared mustard to give it a kick.

Mushroom sauce

Fry sliced mushrooms in a little butter and add to your white sauce at the end. Some Port, soy sauce and dried dill can turn it into a feast.

Tomato pasta sauce

Tomato pasta sauce is not based on Béchamel. To make it, fry up a chopped onion and some crushed garlic in oil, add a few dried herbs of your choice, and then add a can of diced tomatoes. Bring to the boil and simmer for a few minutes. A slug of red wine and a little sugar will bring out the flavour.

Cooking Meat

A general cooking guide

Sometimes when you're at the supermarket looking at the rows of vegetables or the shelves of meat, it can be hard to imagine how you will cook them all. What type of meat do I need for a stir fry? What goes well in a slow cooker? Here's a guide to help you out, with thanks to Kylie Ball and the SHELf team at Deakin Uni[26]

Cooking Method	Suggested Cut of Meat (in order of least to most expensive)	Suggested Vegies & Cooking Method
Stir fry	Beef (sliced rump or fillet) Chicken (thigh or breast with skin off) Lamb (fillet) Pork (fillet)	Stir fry Asian greens (e.g. bok choy), broccoli, bean shoots, cabbage, cauliflower, carrot, capsicum, celery, garlic, ginger, mushrooms, okra, snow peas, zucchini
BBQ/Grill	Beef (porterhouse steak, T-bone steak, scotch fillet) Chicken (wings/nibblets, thigh, breast) Lamb (steak, mid-loin chops, cutlets) Pork (scotch fillet, mid-loin chops, cutlets)	Serve with fresh salads (bean, coleslaw, green or potato) or steamed vegetables such as broccoli, carrot, cauliflower, green beans. Grill on the BBQ: asparagus, corn, eggplant, mushrooms, onions, potatoes (pre-cooked)

Roast	Beef (rump roast, round roast) Chicken (marinaded wings & drumettes*, whole chicken) Lamb (shoulder, leg) Pork (shoulder, leg, ribs)	Roasted beetroot, carrots, eggplant, garlic, parsnip, potatoes, pumpkin, swede, sweet potato, turnips, zucchini or serve with steamed asparagus, beans, broccoli, brussels sprouts, cabbage, cauliflower, corn, peas
Slow Cooker/ casserole	Beef (chuck steak, chump chops, shin/shank) Chicken (drumsticks, Maryland**, whole chicken) Lamb (shanks, leg) Pork (hock, silverside)	In pot, cook meat with asparagus, broad beans, cabbage, capsicum, carrots, celery, corn, garlic, leek, mushrooms, onion, peas, pumpkin, zucchini

*A drumette is the part of a chicken's wing closest to its body. With the tip removed it looks like a little drumstick

**Chicken Maryland is a drumstick with the thigh attached

Barbecues

Everyone thinks that they are the best BBQ-er around – if you put a pair of tongs in someone's hand their ego starts running wild! (It's a bit like driving – ever heard anyone say they're a bad driver?) I'm sure it's not you or me but some of us must be less than perfect, so where better to get information on cooking the perfect steak than from a butcher? With many thanks to Jack Purcell Meats in Brisbane[27] for this information.

First, heat the barbecue to hot before you add the steak. The steak should sizzle as it makes contact with the heat. If you're using a frying pan, preheat it to moderately-high, not hot. If you're cooking a thick steak or like your steak well done, move it to a cooler part of the barbecue or lower the heat to moderately-high as it cooks.

Turn the steak only once. Let it cook on one side until moisture appears on the surface, then turn it over, otherwise it will be tough.

Touch the surface of your steak using your tongs – if it's very soft it's rare. If it's firm, it's well done. Yep, if it's in between it's medium-rare. Over time, you'll work out which 'feel' corresponds with each level of 'doneness'.

Don't forget about residual heat. Your steak will keep cooking once it's off the BBQ.

Resting your meat

One thing to note is that all meat needs time to rest before serving. This means the meat will lose less juice when cut, and will therefore be more succulent and tastier. The time taken to rest will depend on its size: steaks or chops should stand for at least 2 to 3 minutes before serving while a roast is best rested for 10 to 20 minutes before carving.

Which brings me to…

Roast Recipes

A roast will generally be cooked in a moderate oven for 30 minutes per 500g (1 pound) of weight at around 185°C/375°F. So if you are a maths genius like me you will able to work out that a 2kg or 4lb lamb roast will require 2 hours. Generally, you can just chuck a roast in a roasting pan and then into a pre-heated oven and forget about it. Put some peeled potatoes, sweet potatoes, parsnip, pumpkin or onions around the bottom of the pan with some oil, turn them every now and then, and that's your vegies done too.

Make sure you take the meat out of the roasting pan and let it rest and then you can whack up the temperature to crisp the vegies for that last 10-20 minutes.

Lemon-up-the-bottom-chicken

If you want something a bit fancier than a standard roast, how about a 'Lemon-up-the-bottom chicken'? Delicious AND a conversation starter!

Ingredients

1 chicken

2 lemons

Freshly ground black pepper

Method

Turn on the oven to 185°C/350°F. Get a fork and poke deep holes in the lemons all over. Check there is nothing in the chicken's cavity (such as stuffing) – if there is, remove it. Push the lemons up the chicken's bottom. Grind lots of pepper all over the chicken.

Put a very small amount of butter or water in the bottom of the roasting pan, or put the chicken on a roasting rack in the pan so that the chicken doesn't stick. Roast for 1-1½ hours maximum or until, when you insert a knife near the joint of the leg, the juices run clear, not red. Spooning up the juices and pouring them over the chicken while it cooks (i.e. basting) will give you a crispier skin.

Stir fry

If you are really short of time, a stir fry is an excellent solution. You can have this on the table in less than 10 minutes.

Ingredients

Strips of meat (look at the chart earlier in this chapter for which type)
Prepared vegies (ditto)
Oil
One of the following: soy sauce, Kecap Manis (Indonesian Soy Sauce), stock or
prepared stir fry sauce

Method

Heat a tablespoon of oil in a wok or high-sided frying pan, chuck in the strips of meat and fry for a couple of minutes, stirring all the time till they are lightly browned. If you are using onion or garlic, throw them in and fry them for a minute or so, adding a teaspoon of oil if required. Now throw in the rest of the vegies, again adding a teaspoon of oil if required and fry for a couple of minutes. (You can take the meat out and cook the vegetables by themselves to avoid overcooking the meat and then add it back in with the sauce, but I tend to just leave it in there.)

Try a piece of vegetable to check they are done and when they are, add in one of the following:

- A couple of shakes of soy sauce
- A couple of shakes of Kecap Manis
- ½ cup of stock (or ½ cup water with ½ a stock cube dissolved in it)
- A jar or sachet of prepared stir fry sauce

Keep stirring for a minute or so till it's all hot and serve. Eat with rice, potatoes, flat bread or pasta. You can throw cooked rice, potatoes or pasta in near the end if you like.

Pasta Recipes

Spaghetti Bolognaise

You've probably eaten spaghetti bolognaise since you were a little kid and this is why: it's delicious, it's quick, it's cheap and it's reasonably healthy. Here's a recipe, but if you're really short of time, don't be ashamed to buy one of those bottles of pasta tomato sauces designed to be added to meat. Fry some mince till it's lightly brown, breaking it up with the wooden spoon as you go along. Add the sauce, some wine, some grated vegies or red lentils, and enjoy. Lentils in particular are a great addition as they give you more volume and increase the protein level. And they're cheap, too.

So, here's a basic Spag Bol recipe. Go for it!

Basic Spaghetti Bolognaise

Don't be afraid to make this a day or two in advance as it gets better and better. A bit of *flaveur de fridge* can work wonders.

Ingredients

500g/1lb mince (choose the low fat one if you can afford it)
1 onion, chopped
2 garlic cloves, crushed
1 carrot grated
1 zucchini grated
3 rashers of bacon, chopped and fried
½ cup red wine
1 teaspoon of Italian herbs (or just Oregano if you prefer)
1 tablespoon of sugar if required (taste first, depends on the ripeness of the tomatoes)
3 tablespoons of tomato paste
1 tin of chopped tomatoes
½ cup red lentils (optional)

Method

Fry up the onion and garlic for a couple of minutes but don't let them brown, then add the meat and fry for a couple more minutes, breaking it up with a wooden spoon until it's brown. Add all the other ingredients, and some more liquid if it's looking too dry. This can be plain water, or beef stock, or water and a beef stock cube. Boil for as long as you've got – anywhere from five minutes on medium heat, to an hour on low is fine. Serve with any pasta and lots of grated Parmesan cheese.

Easy lasagne

Make a big batch of bolognaise sauce and use it the next day to make a lasagne! This recipe doesn't require you to make a cheesy sauce so it's very easy, but if you're in a bit of a kitchen groove, make the cheese sauce mentioned earlier instead.

Ingredients

Bolognaise sauce
Lasagne sheets
Grated cheese (or cheese sauce)

Method

Fill a large dish with layers of lasagne, meat sauce, and cheese, repeated. Finish with lasagne sheets and sprinkled cheese. It can help to put a light layer of meat sauce on the bottom of the dish to stop it sticking. Cook in an oven heated to 185°C/375°F for around 30 minutes till the top is golden brown and crunchy.

Egg Recipes

Spaghetti Carbonara

There's nothing like a good Spaghetti Carbonara and it's a delicious meal when you don't have much in the cupboard. I've been making this for years, tweaked from an original recipe by Guy Grossi.

Ingredients

150g/5oz pancetta or bacon (can be replaced with ham if that's all you've got)
5 eggs, whisked with a fork
Pepper and salt
2 good handfuls of Parmesan cheese
4 tablespoons of chopped parsley
Spaghetti

Method

Cut up the pancetta into pieces and fry in a deep frying pan. Meanwhile, cook the spaghetti according to the instructions on the packet. Once the pancetta is golden brown, turn off the heat. In a separate bowl break in the eggs and mix in the chopped parsley and most of the Parmesan cheese (leaving some to sprinkle on the top once finished). Season with pepper and salt.

Once the spaghetti is cooked, drain it and return it to the hot pan, then quickly add in the pancetta and the egg mixture. Stir. The residual heat of the pasta will cook the egg slightly and form the sauce. (Look! It's magic!). If it's too cold and the egg is not cooking, you can pop it back on to the stove on low heat for 30 seconds or so. Sprinkle with Parmesan cheese.

Quiche Lorraine

Quiches only take minutes to prepare and an hour to cook; they are so easy you should never be tempted to buy one. Great served warm with a salad for dinner, or cold for lunch or a picnic.

Ingredients

One sheet of frozen short-crust pastry
3 eggs
A couple of slices of bacon
4 slices of Swiss cheese (for a traditional quiche), or a big handful of grated tasty cheese
1 cup milk
½ cup cream

A pinch of nutmeg
Salt and pepper

Method

Heat up the oven to 200°C/400°F. Pull your pastry out of the freezer and let it defrost on the kitchen bench on its piece of separating plastic. Once it's malleable, line the pie dish with the pastry sheet. Given that your pastry sheet will most likely be square and your pie dish will most likely be round you may need to cut off the four corners to patch the other parts of the pastry to fit the pie dish. Make sure you join the pieces well or else the quiche will leak. I think it works best to use a knife to do a little row of cuts across the join – not fully through the pastry but just on the surface, then rub the seam with your finger. Cut off excess pastry level with the top of the pie dish and place the dish in the fridge for around 20 minutes.

Meanwhile, chop your bacon into small pieces and fry it (it won't need fat). Mix in a bowl your eggs, milk, cream, nutmeg, salt and pepper. Take out two tablespoons of this mix and put it into a mug with a tablespoon of flour. Stir this till it's smooth and then put it back into the bowl it came from and stir well.

Put the cooked bacon on the bottom of the pie dish and then the cheese. Pour the egg mixture on top and cook in the oven for 15 minutes, then turn the oven down to 185°C (375°F) and cook until the top is lightly brown and the mixture is set, around 45 minutes.

Yum!

Other quiches

For variations, try any of the following:
- Defrosted frozen spinach (squeeze it out well over the sink)
- Salmon or tuna
- Left-over chopped up vegies
- Feta cheese instead of the Gruyere or tasty cheese
- Caramelised onion and goat's cheese instead of the other cheese
- Anything you've ever tried in a quiche before! Just make sure it's not too wet and you put it in the pastry flan before you put in the milk and egg mix.

Omelettes

An omelette has to be about the quickest meal you can make and it's delicious.

Ingredients

2 eggs
½ tablespoon water
Spray oil

Method

Break 2 eggs into a cup and add the water. Mix this up with a fork. Spray a frying pan with oil, and heat it up till it's medium hot. Pour in the eggs and swirl them round the frying pan till they cover the base. Using a fork, push from the outside edge to the centre, and then tilt the pan towards that spot, allowing the mixture to fill the part of the saucepan that is bare. Do this four or five times.

Turn to medium and allow it to cook for about 2 minutes. (The water you've added into the eggs will turn into steam, fluffing up the omelette). Add chopped cheese, ham, thinly sliced vegies, or anything you like on to the top of half the omelette and leave for another minute or so. Fold the empty half of the omelette over the top of the half with goodies on top, and then slide it on to a plate to serve.

Rice Recipes

Risotto

Risotto is another great dish to prepare – quick, cheap and can be made with whatever you've got on hand in your cupboard. However, you must use Arborio rice which has a high starch content and can absorb masses of liquid to become deliciously creamy but not soggy. Another tip is to grate your own Parmesan. It's so much better than the bought packets of Parmesan which look and taste like sawdust. (I feel I need to clarify at this point that I haven't actually eaten sawdust.)

Ingredients - per person

100g/3oz Arborio rice
A teaspoon of butter
300 mls/1¼ cups liquid (stock, or a mix of stock and wine)
Parmesan cheese

Method

Heat up your stock/wine mix in a saucepan till it is just simmering, and keep it gently bubbling the whole time you are making the risotto. Put the rice and butter into a saucepan and cook, stirring, till the rice is glossy and looking translucent. Not too long! Ladle half a cup of stock into the rice mixture and stir while it bubbles away. Once it's all been absorbed, add some more liquid and stir again. Repeat till all the stock is gone.

Stir in a good handful of Parmesan cheese and any herbs you might have on hand. Sprinkle with Parmesan to serve.

There is no limit to what you can add into your risotto, but here are a couple of ideas:

- ½ teaspoon of saffron and some onion – fry the onion with the rice, and add the saffron half way through the ladling process (this one's called Risotto Milanese)
- Smoked salmon, capers and lemon juice
- Asparagus, peas and lemon juice
- Tomato and ham
- Cooked pumpkin chunks

Fried rice

This is another great classic which doesn't take long to prepare, can be quite nutritious and is cheap.

Ingredients

Left-over cooked rice (or cook some early in the day and leave to cool in the fridge)
Soy Sauce or for a different flavour, use Indonesian Kecap Manis
Oil
Any of the following:

- *Chopped vegies (those frozen chopped ones in a bag are good or anything else you've got on hand)*
- *Tomato*
- *Sliced lettuce (yes weird, but try it!)*
- *Egg*
- *Bacon*
- *Onion*
- *Garlic*
- *Cooked prawns, chicken or pork in small pieces*

Method

Heat up some oil in your large frying pan, add the onion, garlic, bacon or vegies and cook, stirring. Move these to the side of the pan and pour in the egg which you have whisked with a fork in a cup. Cook it in one piece, turn it over with your fish slice and when it is cooked, cut it through using the edge of your fish slice. (You should end up with little ribbons of egg but it doesn't matter what you end up with actually!) Add in the rice, splash on soy sauce until you've got a little bit of colour, and mix everything through together. Cook for another minute or so till the whole dish is hot and serve.

Making Cakes

Everyone should know how to whip up a good cake. These take about 5 minutes to prepare and you can have one ready (well, at least in the oven) from the time someone texts you saying they're on their way till when they ring the doorbell.

- Use eggs at room temperature – you'll get a bigger volume when you beat them resulting in a lighter cake
- Often recipes will ask you to cream together the butter and sugar which means beating them together until the mixture is light in colour and creamy in texture. You then beat in the eggs, and then fold in the flour and milk alternately. This is the correct way to make a cake, and it will give a great texture but we're talking easy here so you can cheat by just melting the butter in a cup and beating it with the other ingredients
- You can then use the left over butter in the cup to paint around the tin with a pastry brush so the cake doesn't stick. If the tin's not made of silicone, line the base with a circle of baking paper as well
- If you are using a fan-forced oven, drop the temperature by 20°C/50°F from that listed in the recipe
- Cook cakes as close to the middle of the oven as you can, and turn the tins around when the cake is set (about 2/3 of the way through the cooking time)
- At the end of the cooking time and if you think the cake might be ready, touch the top of the cake gently. Your finger will bounce back and the cake won't feel gooey if it's cooked. The cake also won't wobble as you slide the rack out of the oven to have a look
- If it feels dry and there's no wobbling, insert a skewer into the cake. If there is goo on the bottom of the skewer when you pull it out, stick the cake back into the oven for another 10 mins or so and then repeat the skewer action. The skewer will come out clean when the cake is cooked
- If the cake splits while cooking, the oven's too hot: if it doesn't rise, the oven isn't hot enough and if it rises then sinks, it's not been cooked long enough.

Cake Recipes

The easiest cake is the famous (at least in our family) Dump & Stir chocolate cake.

Dump and Stir chocolate cake

This recipe has been in my family for generations. It can be adapted to make a whole range of cakes, and the best part is that there is no-one who can't make it. Well, almost.

Ingredients

1 cup sugar
1 cup Self Raising flour
½ cup milk
2 tablespoons cocoa
3 tablespoons butter, melted in a cup
2 eggs
1 teaspoon vanilla (essence, extract, whatever you have)

Method

First turn on the oven to 185° C/350°F. Dump all the ingredients in a bowl. Stir vigorously by hand (or with a mixer) till the mixture gets a bit thicker and lighter in colour. Sometimes because of kitchen gremlins it doesn't and that's fine. Sit your silicon cake tin on an oven tray and brush it with butter. If you are using a metal cake tin, cut out a circle of baking paper to sit on the bottom, and paint the sides with the left over butter.

Cook for around 45 minutes or until a skewer inserted into the middle comes out clean. If there is goo on the bottom of the skewer, stick the cake back into the oven for another 10 mins or so and repeat the skewer action. You can also touch the top of the cake gently and you'll feel if it's cooked – it shouldn't be gooey at all.

Once it's cooked, leave the cake in the pan for 5 minutes, then carefully run a knife around the edge, put a wire cooling rack on top and flip it over so that the cake is now upside down on the rack. Remove the tin. After another 10 minutes, put a plate upside down on the bottom of the cake and flip the whole back up the right way so the cake is now on the plate. Sift icing sugar on the top. Impressive!

Custard cake

Simply replace the cocoa with custard powder. Cook as above.

Orange cake

Leave out the cocoa and add in the grated rind of one orange. Instead of the ½ cup of milk, use ¼ cup milk and ¼ cup orange juice.

Cinnamon apple cake

Leave out the cocoa, and place peeled, cored, and finely sliced apple decoratively on the top. Once it's out of the oven, brush with a little melted butter then sprinkle with 1 tablespoon of caster sugar (or just normal sugar if that's all you've got) mixed with a couple of good shakes of cinnamon.

Tea cake

Leave out the cocoa. When it's hot out of the oven, spread with melted butter and sprinkle with 1 tablespoon of caster sugar (or just normal sugar if that's all you've got) mixed with a couple of good shakes of cinnamon

Cup cakes

Use 1½ cups of Self Raising Flour, instead of 1 cup. Spoon into the holes of a muffin tin which have been brushed with butter. Cook until golden brown and a skewer inserted comes out clean.

Icing

If it's for a special occasion, you can ice your cake quickly and easily.

Ingredients

A generous tablespoon of butter
2 cups icing sugar mix, sifted
Enough milk to make a spreadable paste
Colouring

Method

Put the butter into a bowl and melt it in the microwave. Add the icing sugar mix. You can use pure icing sugar if you like but sometimes it sets hard in the pack and can be difficult to work with. Mix, adding milk tablespoon by tablespoon until you get to a spreadable consistency (a bit like toothpaste).

If you want to have coloured icing, add a few drops of colouring now and mix well. If you want to make pink icing, use only a very little butter at the start, as otherwise it will end up being orange!

Spread this on a COOL cake, starting at the middle of the top and working out towards the edges. You can go down the sides if you have enough icing and are feeling extravagant. If you put icing on a hot cake it will all melt and run onto the plate. Very sad.

A fresh cut flower on top looks very Masterchef or MKR, or you can even just add some candles if it's a birthday.

Pancakes

Weird, but if you want to make pancakes just add a teaspoon of baking powder to the Dump & Stir mixture and leave out the cocoa. (Buy hey, if you want chocolate pancakes, leave it in!) Spray your large frying pan with oil or use melted butter. Pour on mixture to make the size pancake you want and flip when there are bubbles all the way through and the edge of the pancake is dry. Cook only half a minute or so on the other side.

If you are after crepes, use more milk/less flour. If you are after hotcakes, use more flour/less milk. The first pancake is always a mess – supposedly you're meant to give it to the chooks to say thank you for the eggs (but the dog will do).

Chocolate Ripple cake

Here is a recipe for the legendary Australian dessert that everyone has loved since they were little. It's as easy as eating them out of the packet but way more delicious!

Ingredients

One packet of Arnott's Chocolate Ripple biscuits
One small container of whipping cream (the usual cream; if you read the label you'll see it has gelatine added)
1 tablespoon sugar
1 teaspoon vanilla

Method

Beat the cream, vanilla and sugar until the cream has a firm consistency. It should be able to hold a firm peak and be spreadable, not pourable. Spread a little bit of cream on a long serving dish, then take one biscuit in your hand and spread cream on the flat side of it. Stand it up on the dish. Get another biscuit, spread the flat side with cream, and stand it up next to the first one. Continue until you have used up all the biscuits.

The only trick here is to make sure you put enough cream between the biscuits so they stick to each other and go soft, but leave enough to completely cover the log, which you do now. Now put it into the fridge to 'soggify'. If you are waiting more than a couple of hours, cover it with cling wrap. When you cut it, make sure you slice it on the diagonal so you get a pretty layered look with each piece. YUM!

If you are short of time, you can dip each biscuit in some milk first before spreading with cream, which will decrease the amount of time required for it to go soggy. Make sure you dip quickly as otherwise you'll end up with a crumbly, milky mess. You could also experiment with dipping the biscuits in coffee or alcohol for a change.

Cookie Recipes

There's really only one cookie or biscuit that we need to include here. Not very complicated but oh! so delicious!

Choc-chip cookies

Ingredients

125g/4½ oz butter
½ cup sugar
½ cup brown sugar
1 teaspoon vanilla
1 egg
½ cup quick oats
1½ cups Self Raising flour
½ teaspoon salt
125g/4½ oz choc chips (white, milk or dark or a mixture), or crushed up bits of left-over chocolate

Method

Turn on the oven to 185°C/375°F. Beat the butter, sugars and vanilla together till the mixture is smooth and creamy. Add the egg and beat again. Don't worry if it curdles and looks a bit lumpy. Stir in the flour, quick oats and salt, and finally mix in the chocolate chips. This step will be hard as the mixture will be firm.

Form into balls a bit smaller than the size of cookie you want and place them on a baking tray lined with baking paper. Leave a nice gap between them, as they will spread.

Bake for around 12-15 minutes, until they are golden brown and the top of each biscuit is slightly set. Make sure they are still a bit soft as biscuits continue to firm up as they cool and what looks like a great texture in the oven can become rock hard once they cool. After 5 minutes out of the oven, use a fish slice to gently lift them and place them on a cooling rack to firm up.

Okay, for those of you who really want some variations, here are two:

Plain cookies

You can leave out the choc-chips but really, have you thought this through? Decorate the top with half a maraschino cherry. Or instead of the cherries, once cool, dip half of each biscuit in melted chocolate.

Fruit cookies

Use sultanas or chopped up dried apricots instead of the choc-chips.

Scone Recipes

It is very impressive when your parents or someone else you want to amaze comes round to afternoon tea for the first time, and you are bringing some scones out of the oven. Nice job! This recipe works and it's easy.

Turn your oven on to hot – 220°C/420°F. If it's a fan-forced oven it should be 20°C/50°F lower.

Ingredients

4 cups Self Raising flour (not plain)
250 mls (that's one cup) of lemonade
250 mls normal cream (NOT the really thick spoonable stuff)
A pinch of salt

Method

Mix this all together with a knife (yep, a knife. Go figure.) Add a bit more flour if it's a bit sticky. Once it's together put it on the kitchen bench onto which you've sprinkled some flour and knead very, very gently. If you knead too roughly or for too long you will end up with a tough texture. Push it out flat till it's about 3cm thick and cut it into rounds. It can help to dip your cutter into flour each time before you cut but you still might have to shake the cutter to release the dough.

Place each scone on to a tray lined with baking paper so they are touching (this means they rise up instead of spreading out) and cook in a really hot oven till they are golden brown, around 15 minutes. Keep an eye on them because your oven is on full blast.

Eat with whipped cream and some home-made jam that you've also made yourself. You're so remarkable!

Jam & Chutney Recipes

Contrary to what most people think, jam is really easy to make, doesn't require any exotic ingredients or equipment, and is extremely impressive.

Pectin

Jam needs something called pectin in order to set – some fruits like plums or quinces are high in pectin so will set very easily by themselves, others have medium pectin (like raspberries) so need a little bit of help, and some like strawberries have very little so you can boil it till the cows come home and it still won't want to set. Also, unripe fruit has higher pectin than ripe fruit, so if your fruit is very ripe, it'll need help to set. Pectin is found in a number of ingredients but lemon juice, rind or seeds are often at hand and easy to use.

Other no-fail options include commercial Jam Setta, Citric Acid, Tartaric Acid and jam sugar, which are all available in the baking aisle of the supermarket.

Jars, lids & labels

Save your old jars, especially if they have plain metal lids as these look best to give as gifts once filled with your jam. Don't use rusty lids as they are hard to sterilise and don't give a good seal. Soak the labels off your jars but if they don't come off easily, either use Eucalyptus oil to help, or try another jar. Then put them through a dishwasher, or give them a good wash in hot soapy water. Rinse in clean water and let air dry. One interesting thing to note is that there are only around four sizes of lids, so you can mix and match to get jars (with no labels or residual glue) and lids (with no printing).

You'll need to label your jars with what's inside, your name and the date you made it. Go on! Take the credit! There's no need to buy jam labels from a cookware shop although they can be enticing – office labels run through a printer can be just as effective and sticky. (And while we're at it – what's brown and sticky? Answer: a stick.) You can tie a little brown cardboard label on with ribbon, or if your lid looks terrible, you can cut out circles of fabric to put on the top with a rubber band. Very 1950s.

Sterilising jars

When you are ready to make your jam, pull the jars out of the cupboard and wash them again in hot soapy water, rinse them, then let them drain upside down on a tea towel till they are almost dry. Do the same for the lids. Turn your oven to low (100°C/200°F). Place the jars right side up on a baking tray and put them in the oven. Once your jam is ready, take the jars out of the oven and put the lids into the oven in their place. By the time you have filled your jars, your lids will be hot and sterile and ready to place on the jars. Use a tea towel to tighten the lids – they'll be hot!

Be careful when you are filling the jars and try to avoid spilling jam over the thread of the jar or down its side. I always ladle the jam into a heatproof jug to pour into my jars – if you don't have a ladle, use a cup. If you are making lots of jam, invest in a jam funnel – it will keep your jars and your bench clean and make you feel like a professional! They only cost a couple of dollars. If you do spill jam on the edge of a jar, clean it up with a damp piece of kitchen paper or a tissue before you put the lid on. Don't be tempted to use your grotty kitchen sponge. You are trying to keep the jars sterile!

Setting point

To test if jam is set, place a saucer in the freezer and leave it there for around 5-10 minutes. Take it out of the freezer and place a half tablespoon of the hot jam onto it. Return to the freezer for a minute or so, pull it out then press your finger against the edge of the blob. If it's set and wrinkles when pressed, it's done. (Another way is to run your finger through the blob – if it joins up again it's not ready but if stays in 2 separate blobs it is).

Raspberry jam

So here we go – this is one of the easiest jams to make and so tasty!

1 kg/2lbs sugar

1 kg/2lbs fresh or frozen raspberries

Juice of a lemon

Method

Preheat the oven to 100°C/200°F. Place a saucer into the freezer. (Yes, do as I say!) Place clean washed jam jars on a tray and put them in the oven. Microwave the sugar gently to warm it. It should just feel warm through the packet, not hot.

Meanwhile, place the raspberries and lemon juice into a pan and bring to the boil, lightly crushing them to draw out some juice. Cook for about two minutes, then add the sugar to the raspberries and stir well. Cook for 6-8 minutes, stirring frequently. Skim off any scum from the surface of the jam with a spoon and discard. The skimming aims to give you a clearer result but I only do it if I can be bothered or there's a lot of it.

Test for setting point (see earlier). If it's not ready, return the jam to the heat and cook for a further 5-10 minutes before testing again. You'll need to keep a good eye on it as at this stage it can start to catch on the bottom and burn.

When the jam is done, pull out the jars from the oven and put the lids into the oven on another tray. Remove the jam from the heat and pour it into the sterilised jars. Put the lids on while still hot. Use a tea towel to tighten the lids.

Strawberry Jam

Ingredients

1kg/2lbs strawberries, fresh (washed and hulled) or frozen
1kg/2lbs sugar
2 or 3 lemons or use Jam Setta*

Method

Make as Raspberry Jam, above. I personally prefer frozen strawberries as it's so much easier. If you go for fresh, remember that unripe strawberries which are high in pectin will set more easily; ripe strawberries will give you a better flavour but the jam will be hard to set. Catch 22.

You may need to cook this for up to 15 minutes – much longer and you risk the jam losing its flavour and becoming darker in colour. If you find the jam is not setting easily, add more lemon juice. Once it has reached setting point (see earlier), bottle in sterilised jars (ditto) as per the Raspberry Jam recipe.

*Jam Setta is available in the baking section of the supermarket. Follow the instructions on the packet

Cumquat marmalade

Cumquats are the little orange citrus fruit found through the Asia-Pacific region in people's gardens, and that are abundant in Chinese areas in the Lunar New Year (they symbolise good luck). While some people eat them whole, I think you'd have to be pretty desperate to eat one as it's like eating a lemon raw. But they are sublime made into marmalade so if you happen to come across some, grab them! Cumquat marmalade makes an excellent and meaningful gift to have on hand for grandparents or other oldies – even your parents will probably love it.

Wash the cumquats and then freeze them in a plastic bag. You can leave them in the freezer for months until you have the time to make this jam. Pull them out of the freezer and when they are half defrosted, cut each one in half and then cut that half into about four slices. (The reason I do it while half frozen is that you don't lose so much juice, they're easier to cut than when fresh and the time in the freezer will have softened the skins so they take less time to cook). If you have time, put them in a bowl, add water so the cumquats are just covered, and leave overnight; if you're in a rush, you can cook straight away.

Measure out the mixture in cups into a saucepan and add the same number of cups of sugar. Bring to a gentle boil and as the skins break down and release the seeds, remove the seeds with a spoon. (These all rise to the surface.) Boil for around 15 minutes to half an hour and then test for setting point (see page 108), at which stage the mixture will be slightly thicker. If not yet at setting point, keep boiling and testing, and once setting point has been reached, bottle in sterilised jars (see page 109). Label. Enjoy!

Tomato chutney

Chutney's not so hard to make either, and can turn a humble meat pie into something a little more stylish (or at least more edible). It can also work miracles with a slab of tasty cheese and some fresh bread. You can find chutney recipes everywhere but this is the one I like – from the Broadford Kindergarten's

1970 fundraising cookbook, so while it's probably not that fashionable, it has certainly stood the test of time!

Ingredients

1.5kg/3lbs ripe tomatoes
500g/1lb onions
400g/14oz sugar
1 tablespoon mild curry powder
1½ tablespoons mustard
2 tablespoons flour
Salt and pepper to taste
Brown vinegar

Method

First you need to peel the tomatoes. The easiest way to do this is to cut crosses on their bottoms and then put them into boiling water for a short time (try 30 seconds to start with). You will see that the skins start to wrinkle and they can be peeled off with your fingers, starting at the cut crosses. It can be easier on your hands to put them into cold water before you peel the skins. Once peeled, dice them, add the peeled and sliced onions and sprinkle with some salt; let this sit overnight.

Next day, put into a saucepan with enough vinegar to cover and boil for one hour. Add the sugar. Put the other dry ingredients into a cup and add a little of the liquid from the chutney to moisten, then add to the tomatoes and onions. Boil for another hour or until it thickens, then bottle into sterilised jars (see page 108 for how to sterilise a jar).

Five Top Tips

1. Make sure you rest your meat when it comes out of the oven or off the BBQ. It will be more tender and much juicier

2. All you have to do to cook a roast is put it in the oven for 30 minutes per 500g/1lb of weight at 185°C/375°F. Nothing hard about that

3. If your cake splits when cooking, the oven was too hot. If it sinks when it comes out of the oven, it wasn't cooked long enough. And if it's flat, you either used the wrong flour or the oven was too cold

4. Scones are quick and easy to make, but there are two rules for success: don't stir them too much and make sure your oven is really hot

5. You need to sterilise your jars for making jam. Wash and dry them, then heat them in a low-temperature oven while you cook the jam. Easy.

CHAPTER 7

I DON'T FEEL SO WELL...

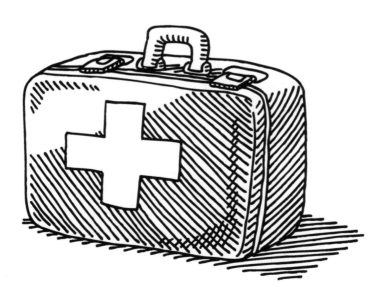

Now that you are out on your own and don't have your mum nagging you ("Have you had your breakfast?" "What time did you get to bed last night?" "Are you eating enough fruit and vegies?"), perhaps it's time that you started thinking seriously about your own health. The little things you do every day can make a big difference overall to how well you feel and how much you can achieve in your day-to-day life. So, sit back and relax, and read on to find out how you can manage your own health.

Haven't Got Time To Read The Whole Chapter? Read This.

1. If you're feeling sad or anxious, or think you may have an eating disorder, seek help. Contact Beyond Blue, Headspace or The Butterfly Foundation. It's free and you can remain anonymous if you want

2. Keep healthy by having 30 minutes of exercise most days, eating lean meat, lots of fruit and vegies, and drinking water in preference to anything else

3. RICE is the best way to treat a sprain: Rest, Ice, Compression and Elevation. If there is severe pain, bruising or loss of function, see your doctor

4. Chlamydia is the most frequently reported notifiable condition in Australia[28]. Treatment is two antibiotic tablets. Even if you have no symptoms, if you are sexually active do a wee test at your doctor's every year

5. When you clean your teeth, if what you spit out is pink, you may have gum disease (gingivitis). You need to clean your teeth better and floss every day. If it continues, see your dentist.

How To Keep Healthy

Did you know that scientists have discovered meat pies and chips are a healthy diet? Nah, only kidding.

Checklist: Healthy eating

Sadly the truth is that the Australian Dietary Guidelines[29] indicate you need to do the following:
- Have 30 minutes of moderate exercise on most days
- Eat lean meat, chicken and fish, tofu, nuts, legumes and eggs (2.5-3 serves a day)
- Eat lean dairy products (2.5 serves a day)
- Have lots of different coloured vegies (5 serves a day) and fruits (2 serves a day)
- Eat wholegrain carbohydrates & cereals (6 serves a day)
- Eat oily fish which is high in Omega-3 fatty acids
- Drink water in preference to soft drinks or fruit juices
- Don't drink too much alcohol (less than 2 standard drinks per day)
- Limit salty foods, saturated fats, sugar and processed foods.

Are you at risk from a weight related health issue? One way to know is to grab a tape measure and put it around your waist – if your waist is over 80cm (as a woman) or 94cm (as a man) you may be. It's not unusual to put on weight once you leave the confines of home or school, so if this is a problem for you, have a look at the *Measure Up* website[30]. This has been put together by the Australian Government and aims to help you manage your weight. But remember – we're talking about health here and not about trying to look like someone in the media. Love yourself, don't compare yourself to others and do things that you enjoy doing. You are more than what you look like ☺

In Your First Aid Kit

Things will go wrong with your health however careful you are, so make sure you have a well-stocked first aid kit available when you move out of home.

Checklist: First aid kit

- An antiseptic – choose one of a cream (e.g. Savlon), a dilutable liquid (e.g. Dettol) or a liquid (e.g. Betadine)
- Adhesive strip dressings (e.g. Bandaids)
- A pain killer such as Paracetomol (e.g. Panadol)
- An anti-inflammatory such as Ibuprofen (e.g. Nurofen, for headaches, period pain or migraine)

- Anti-histamine tablets (e.g. for hayfever or allergies)
- A 1% steroid cream – this anti-itch cream is available at the chemist and is great to use when you have an insect bite or rash
- A compression bandage (elastic bandage, ACE bandage) – for musculoskeletal injuries that require compression and support. Don't get this confused with one of those flimsy crepe bandages that is used to keep dressings on
- Wound dressings of different sizes
- An eye bath (that little plastic oval cup on a tiny stem – a bit like a squished egg cup)
- Condoms – okay, maybe these aren't quite in the first aid box, but if you are sexually active or likely to be, have some stashed somewhere.

Home Remedies

Yesterday you felt fine, but today something weird is going on. Your throat's feeling scratchy, or you have sprained your wrist, or you lost a tooth (hopefully not all at the same time). Here's what you need to do:

Coughs and colds

To avoid getting a cold, try to keep yourself healthy (see the drill above: eat well and exercise regularly and also get enough sleep), wash your hands frequently with soap (those nasty cold germs are lurking everywhere), and avoid touching your eyes, nose and mouth. If you do succumb, try the following:

- Get plenty of rest. Take time out from work or study and avoid spreading the misery to all your friends
- Keep your fluids up – clear soup (even from a tin) is good, as is tea or warm water with lemon squeezed into it
- Take a decongestant tablet or spray to clear your nose
- Take a pain killer for headaches and a sore throat
- Try gargling with salty warm water, or dissolved Aspro Clear every four hours (spit it out, don't swallow it). Aspro has the added benefit of being an anti-inflammatory, directly hitting the spot where it's needed
- Try inhalations by putting a towel over your head and breathing in the steam from a bowl of boiling water. Old fashioned but it works a treat.

See a doctor if you continue to have a fever or are not improving after 3-4 days.

Sprains and strains

If you injure yourself and have a sprain or strain, remember **RICE:**

Rest the injured part. Stop doing anything that aggravates it, which could include playing competitive sport, taking exercise classes or running. Don't try to push through the pain as you could increase the damage.

Ice - apply any of the following for 15 minutes, followed by at least a 15 minute break:

- Ice or an ice pack wrapped in a tea towel
- Ice and water in a zip-lock bag wrapped in a tea towel
- A paper cup with water frozen in it and kept in the freezer for this purpose. Peel off the top part of the cup to expose the ice, hold on to the bottom part, and rub it on the site (an ice massage)
- Continue this as required for up to 24 hours after the injury, after which time there will be little further benefit. Do not leave ice directly on the injured part as it is too cold and can cause injury to the skin.

Compression – apply a compression bandage to help minimise swelling.

Elevation – keep the injured part higher than the heart.

If required, take some pain-relieving medication such as Paracetamol. If severe pain continues or there is significant bruising or loss of function, seek medical advice.

Burns

- Remove the source of the burn from the patient, or vice versa
- Do one of the following for 20 minutes: place the burn under cold running water, immerse the affected part in a bucket of cold water or apply a Burnaid dressing. Burnaid dressings are designed for the safe and effective treatment of burns and are not to be confused with normal dressings. Never apply anything else such as butter, Aloe Vera, ice packs, toothpaste (yep, some people do) or any sort of cream
- See the doctor if the burn is very painful, or involves the face, hands, genitals or joints. Call an ambulance (yep, it's 000 in Australia, 911 in the U.S., 112 in Europe and 999 in the U.K.) if the burn involves the eyes or is larger in area than half your arm
- Take a pain killer
- If after a few days, see the doctor if the burn shows any sign of infection. This could be increasing redness, pain, or the development of a sort of furry crust.

Cuts and bleeding

- Apply pressure with a clean pad (e.g. a tea-towel). If nothing is available, use your hand or someone else's hand
- Elevate the affected part
- Keep calm and still for at least the first 10 minutes
- If blood soaks through the pad, don't take it off but apply another one on top
- Seek medical care if you cannot control the bleeding or the cut is very deep.

Knocked-out tooth

If you lose a tooth, wash it in saliva and replace it into the mouth, trying not to touch the root of the tooth. You can use aluminium foil to keep it in place. If you can't replace it, store it in milk, sterile saline or spit, or wrap it in Glad Wrap. You can also store it in your mouth, next to the cheek. Seek immediate dental advice as you have the greatest chance of saving the tooth if you can replant it within 15-20 minutes.

Period pain

- Apply local heat (e.g. a hot water bottle or a heat pack)
- Take Ibuprofen (Nurofen)
- Do some exercise (weird but it can help).

If this is a persistent problem, interfering with your ability to carry out day-to-day activities, speak to your doctor who may recommend going on the contraceptive pill.

Hangovers

These are best avoided of course! Der. Try to drink a glass of water before you start drinking alcohol (so you are not using the alcohol to quench your thirst) and then alternate a soft-drink or water with each glass of alcohol. If you do end up with a hangover, try these steps:

- Rehydrate – drinks lots of water, preferably before you go to bed
- Take some Panadol (not Aspirin as this can irritate the stomach further)
- Have food with sugar – this can help if you have the shakes
- Drink thin soup which gives you nutrients but won't upset your stomach further
- DO NOT have a 'hair of the dog' (i.e. avoid alcohol until you are completely recovered).

Going To See The Doctor

Choosing a doctor

Going to see a doctor can be daunting, particularly if you are a bit coy about what's brought you along. It's good to establish a relationship with a doctor, and if you haven't really clicked with the one you've been seeing as a younger person, try a few others till you find someone you are happy to go and see.

What is bulk billing?

A doctor who 'bulk bills' is easier on your pocket as the government pays the doctor directly for around 90% of the cost of the consultation, and you only pay the balance.

Usually a bulk-billing doctor will have this advertised on their surgery sign or you can ask if they will bulk bill you. Some doctors, who normally do not bulk bill, will do so if you ask nicely, particularly if you are a student.

The downside of a bulk billing doctor is that they can get very busy and often have short appointment times to maximise through-put of patients. At times it can also be hard to get an appointment with them.

Most Common Health Issues For Young Adults

The most common reasons for young people to see a doctor include mental health issues, sexually transmitted diseases, contraception and pap smears, coughs and colds, infections and injuries. Here's how they'll normally be treated.

Mental health issues

According to the 2007 National Survey of Mental Health and Wellbeing, an estimated 671,100 or 26% of young people aged 16-24 were suffering from a mental disorder[31]. These include depression, anxiety and eating disorders. If you think you may be affected, please don't suffer alone. These disorders are very common, the doctor will not think you are weird in any way and they are also treatable by medication and other therapies. You can go and see psychologists or other professionals without seeing your GP first, but it can be a good idea to start at your local doctor's clinic as the Australian Government offers 6-10 partly-subsidised counselling sessions per year under their Mental Health Care Plan. You need a referral from a GP to get the subsidy, so start there. It's also a good idea to rule out a physical reason for the way you're feeling.

But if you're not yet up to seeing someone about what's worrying you, why not have a go at e-treatment? These two websites not only have excellent information, but you can work your way through treatment programmes in the privacy of your own home. These are Australian websites, but of course you can access them from anywhere in the world.

- *Mental Health Online* at www.mentalhealthonline.org.au
- The Centre for Clinical Interventions' Consumer Resources Section at http://www.cci.health.wa.gov.au/resources/consumers.cfm.

The following organisations' websites are also highly recommended:

- *Headspace* (the National Youth Mental Health Foundation)
- *The Butterfly Foundation* (for eating disorders)
- *Youth Beyond Blue* (for depression and anxiety).

CASE STUDY: TACKLE MENTAL HEALTH ISSUES EARLY

Ed had been feeling a bit flat for about a year and his marks at uni were beginning to suffer. He still went out with his mates, but wasn't really enjoying himself and tended to drink too much to compensate. He found that he was sleeping a lot and also had the occasional thought about suicide. He felt that he didn't want to speak to his parents or friends as it felt a bit weird and he didn't want them to think he was crazy.

Finally a friend realised what was going on and convinced him to talk to his GP who didn't think he was weird at all and wrote up a treatment plan, referring him to a counsellor. After two months of sessions, and also reading up a bit on the Headspace website, he began to feel there was light at the end of the tunnel. In hindsight, he wished that he'd got on to it earlier.

Lesson: If you think you might have a mental health issue, take a deep breath and go and see someone about it. You'll be glad you did

---

Sexually transmitted diseases

More than half (around 57%) of all sexually transmissible infections notified in Australia are among 15-24 year olds[32]. These include Gonorrhoea, Syphilis, HIV and Chlamydia.

Gonorrhoea, Syphilis and HIV – see a doctor if you notice a genital discharge or rash, particularly after unprotected sex, or if someone you are in a sexual relationship with has been diagnosed with one of these diseases. Antibiotics are used to treat Gonorrhoea and Syphilis; HIV is treated with anti-viral drugs.

Chlamydia

The incidence of Chlamydia has increased three-fold between 2001 and 2011 according to the Bureau of Statistics[33]. Chlamydia produces no symptoms in either males or females, but can cause infertility in females. If you are sexually active you should be tested every year; testing is simple and only involves a urine test. Treatment is also simple – two antibiotic tablets for you and your partner if the test is positive. See the doctor if someone you are in a sexual relationship with is diagnosed with this disease.

CASE STUDY: CHLAMYDIA

Simone had been a bit of a wild child when she moved into the workforce, and had quite a few short-term relationships. She didn't like condoms and thought that as she had no symptoms, all was well. Ten years later she was married and it was proving difficult to get pregnant. She was tested and found out that she had contracted chlamydia at some stage which now meant that she was infertile. While a simple course of the antibiotic Doxycycline cleared up the infection, she was faced with having no children. She wished someone had told her that she should have had a urine to test for Chlamydia every year as soon as she became sexually active.

Lesson: Get tested every year for Chlamydia if you are sexually active

---

Pap smears

If you are female, over 25 and have ever been sexually active, you need to have a PAP smear every two years, even if you have been immunised with the HPV vaccine. This can be done in a couple of minutes by your GP.

Coughs and colds

Most colds are caused by viruses that do not respond to antibiotics and the doctor will recommend rest, fluids and chemist medications to ease the symptoms. Sometimes you may have a secondary infection, particularly if you are asthmatic, which may require antibiotics.

Sports injuries

If severe pain continues after an injury, and/or there is a lot of bruising and/or movement is severely restricted, seek medical advice. Your GP may refer you for an x-ray to rule out a broken bone or to a physiotherapist, sports medicine specialist or orthopaedic surgeon for further treatment.

Glandular fever

If you have had more than a week or two of fatigue and a sore throat, you should see your GP to rule out Glandular Fever (Infectious Mononucleosis). This is diagnosed by a blood test and treatment largely involves rest. The doctor can provide assistance if you need to ask for special consideration from work or study.

Appendicitis

Appendicitis is common and symptoms include central abdominal pain radiating to the right, loss of appetite, nausea and fever. Treatment involves removing the appendix by surgery.

Torsion of the testes

This can be an incredibly painful condition where one testis (testicle or 'ball') twists inside the scrotum and cuts off its own blood supply. Apart from pain, the testis can also be swollen. This is a medical emergency and you will require surgery to have it corrected.

Contraception

Talk to your GP, a pharmacist or a contraception clinic. Two popular options are:

- Condoms (can be embarrassing to buy but are cheap, you don't need to see a doctor and – this is a big point, so listen up! – they provide protection against sexually transmitted diseases such as HIV as well as Hepatitis B and Chlamydia)
- The contraceptive pill (easy to use and can help with other problems such as painful periods, but you need to get a prescription and they don't protect against STDs).

Other forms of contraception include:

- An IUD (Intra-uterine device) or IUS (Intra-uterine system)
- Implants (e.g. Implanon) or injections
- A diaphragm, cap or female condom
- Natural family planning methods such as looking at changes in vaginal mucus, keeping a diary of when you may be ovulating, or taking your temperature
- Emergency contraception. If you've had unprotected sex you can take the 'morning after pill'. You need to see a doctor to get this and ideally

it should be taken within 24 hours of unprotected sex. After this its effectiveness drops off.

Ideally, sort out which form of contraception you might consider using before you are in the position of needing to use it. Look at a reliable source for further information, such as the *Family Planning Clinic* website.

If you are embarrassed to see your usual GP, remember that as part of patient confidentiality they will never reveal to anyone else (parents included) that you have been to see them about this matter. Alternatively, if you would prefer to be more anonymous, type 'contraceptive clinic' into your Internet browser to find somewhere near you that can help. For example, Family Planning Australia has an Action Centre and drop-in clinic in Melbourne specifically for young people under the age of 25.

Immunisations

In terms of immunisations, by the time you leave home, you are pretty well off the hook. However, there are two things to think about – if you are sexually active, you should have a Chlamydia test every year. It is a simple urine test and it is easily treatable. You should also have a Tetanus booster every 10 years. In Australia this is done at the age of fifteen, so think about this when you turn 25.

Medicare

Medicare is an Australian Government health care system funded by a 2% tax on your salary. Medicare gives all citizens and permanent residents a number of benefits including:

- Heavily subsidised doctor visits if your doctor 'bulk bills'
- Smaller rebates on the cost of visiting your doctor if they do not 'bulk bill'
- Subsidised prescriptions
- Free public hospital treatment
- Free x-rays and blood tests
- After hours medical advice for urgent enquiries on the new GP helpline on 1800 022 222. (For emergencies, in Australia you should still call '000').

Medicare is not the same as health insurance (see further on in this chapter).

How do I get a Medicare card?

Once you turn 15 you can get your own Medicare card. Visit the Medicare[34] website to download the form and then go to a Medicare Centre. You'll need to provide original identification, such as a passport, student card or birth certificate, and also the number of your original (probably parents') Medicare card. While you are there, register your bank account details so that rebates can be paid directly into your account.

How does the rebate system work?

First you need to pay your doctor's bill. Most surgeries will then submit your claim for you as long as you have previously registered your bank details with Medicare. Your rebate will automatically be paid to you by the method you selected when you gave them your details (e.g. by direct deposit or by cheque to your home address).

Otherwise you can claim from Medicare on-line or via an App (just search for 'Medicare' at the App Store). You will need to have registered with *MyGov* but this is a simple process you can do at the MyGov website. The app includes the facility for photographing the receipt and submitting it, again with payment directly into your account. Very cool!

Otherwise you can always go into a Medicare Centre to claim your refund on the spot, or post in one of their forms (again, available on line). You will receive your rebate either as a direct deposit or a payment into your account.

You need to know that there will be a so-called 'gap' between the price the doctor charges you to visit (around $80) and the amount you get back from Medicare (around $30). This $50 'gap' comes out of your own pocket unless you go to a bulk-billing doctor, where the gap is less than $10.

Health Insurance

Health Insurance is not government funded – this is something that you take out yourself to cover two things: hospital treatment, and non-medical specialists such as dentistry, physiotherapy, optometry and radiology. Health Insurance does not cover the 'gap' above.

If you are a full-time student, you may well be covered by your parents' health insurance until you turn 25, so check before you look into taking out your own insurance.

There are a large number of companies offering health insurance, the vast majority of which will sign you up over the Internet. Google a comparison website such as *Compare The Market*[35] to see what each company charges and what they offer.

Three ways to decrease your health insurance costs are:

1. Opt for a high excess for hospital visits. This means every time you go into hospital you will need to make a payment yourself (e.g. $1000), and the higher this is, the lower your annual insurance charge will be

2. Look for a package that has fewer of the extras that you don't need, such as optometry, orthodontic treatment and obstetrics care

3. If you can, pay the whole annual charge up front. Some companies will charge you extra to pay by the month.

When you sign up for health insurance you will get a health insurance card, which you should present when you pay the bill for the non-medical specialist or at the hospital. The receptionist will then be able to claim from your insurance company for you on the spot, and you will just need to pay the difference.

So – is that clear? For doctors, x-rays and blood tests, claim from Medicare. For other non-medical specialists like dentists and physios, and for private hospitals, claim from your own health insurance.

Private hospitals versus public hospitals

Hospitals generally fall into two categories: private and public (although just to confuse things you can be a private patient in a public hospital!). There are a few differences between them.

With private hospitals:
- You must have private health insurance with hospital cover
- You can choose which hospital you go to
- You will not need to go on a waiting list for non-emergency hospital treatment and minor elective surgery such as having your tonsils removed
- You may be able to have a private room
- Generally you will be able to choose the doctor or surgeon that you would like to treat you
- You will need to pay a gap fee to the hospital, and there will be a charge for the surgeon and the anaesthetist if you need them.

With public hospitals:
- You do not have to have private health insurance
- You will not be charged for treatment in the hospital
- You will have limited choices (room, doctor, admission date), but this does not mean that the care will be any worse. For some really serious issues such as after a car accident, public hospitals can offer the best care available
- If it is an emergency, head to a public hospital.

Medicare levy surcharges

One thing to note: the Australian Federal Government encourages people to take out hospital cover by imposing a Medicare Levy Surcharge (in addition to the standard 2% levy) on high earners. There is no surcharge up to an annual taxable income of $84,000, but after that there is a sliding scale of up to an additional 1.5% payable on higher salaries if you don't have hospital cover.

Dental problems affecting young people

Cavities

Here's a weird but true fact: leaving home can be bad for your teeth. There are a whole lot of reasons including:

- Your diet going out the window, with you eating and drinking more sugary products
- Your oral hygiene becoming less strict
- Your level of socialising increasing so you are drinking more sugary and acidic alcohol and not drinking enough water.

All this increases your risk of plaque and you may end up with cavities, which can be very painful and not so attractive. See your dentist regularly for check-ups and if you notice any problems in between times, get it sorted out sooner rather than later. This way you may avoid root and nerve problems, and eventually lost teeth.

Gum disease

When you clean your teeth, if what you spit out is pink, you may have gum disease (gingivitis). Although it is reasonably common, this is not normal and is usually the result of poor oral hygiene so make sure you clean your teeth well (see page 129) and go visit your friendly dentist regularly!

If untreated, gum disease can lead to periodontal disease and tooth loss. Also, in the longer term the bugs causing gum disease can affect both your ability to get pregnant or can result in a premature pre-term birth. They have also been linked to poor heart health.

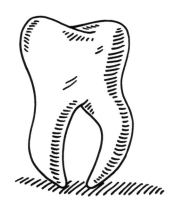

Eruption of wisdom teeth

One thing your dentist will keep an eye on at your regular visits will be your wisdom (3rd molar) teeth, which normally come through between the ages of 17-25. Sometimes they can cause grief when they are impacted (not descending properly and hitting other teeth nearby) or they can become partially descended and then infected. Often there is significant pain. Any of these reasons may indicate that they require removal, which can be done either in the dentist's chair with a local anaesthetic, or you may need a general anaesthetic.

Sports and teeth

Sport is great for your general health but can be bad for your teeth! Apart from the risk of losing a tooth, you may end up drinking a lot of sports drinks, which are not recommended by dentists as they are very sweet and very acidic. If you really have to drink them, rinse your mouth out with water as soon as you can. (But on the other hand, avoid dehydration as this can cause decay due to inadequate saliva to wash and neutralise the acid in your mouth).

Mouthguards are important if you are playing a contact sport, and custom-made is best as they fit well. They are expensive but may be partly subsidised by your health insurance, and as an adult your mouth doesn't change shape so you can keep them for a number of years. That is unless you put them through a hot wash but even then they might survive! Ones from the chemist that you mould in hot water are better than nothing, but they may be uncomfortable and won't sit well over your teeth, meaning a lower level of protection and the risk of choking.

Other Dental Issues

Much of the following information is adapted from *The Young Person's Oral Survival Guide*, with thanks to the Australian Dental Assocation[36].

Tooth whitening

Be careful using tooth whitening kits – they may not be suitable for everyone and the bleach in them can cause permanent side effects such as burns, uneven tooth colour and increased oral sensitivity. See your dentist if you want whiter teeth. (There are new regulations around the type of whitening products that can be bought over the counter or supplied/applied by a non-dentist, so the ADA does not recommend that you do it yourself or go to a beauty therapist to have your teeth whitened).

Orthodontic treatment

If you have always hated the shape of your teeth, you can still have braces as an adult. You'll need to see your regular dentist who can advise you on the best option – this may include a referral to an orthodontist. (Some dentists provide orthodontic treatment themselves.) Treatment time is different in each case but can take a number of years.

Binge drinking

Binge drinking is not a great thing. It can cause you to make questionable decisions, it's bad for your health and get this: it's even crap for your teeth! It not only exposes your teeth to the sugar and acid found in alcoholic drinks, but it also increases the likelihood that you will forget to clean your teeth before you go to bed. Try to rinse your mouth out with water after every alcoholic drink, chew sugar-free gum and clean your teeth before you go to bed, Leaving a toothbrush on your pillow can help to remind you about cleaning.

Vomiting as a result of binge drinking floods your mouth with acid. If you are in any condition to do so, try to remember to clean your teeth or at least rinse out your mouth with water afterwards.

Smoking

There are three main mouth problems caused by smoking:
- Smoking can disguise tooth and gum damage. Damaged gums are normally red and they bleed easily when brushed, but damaged gums belonging to smokers do not. Smoking can therefore make it difficult for dentists to diagnose problems
- The nicotine in smoke affects saliva production. Saliva helps prevent damage from acids so this benefit may be diminished in smokers
- Finally, smoking is the leading cause of oral cancer.

If you can, stop smoking. If you can't, be careful with your brushing and flossing and make sure you see your dentist regularly.

Piercings

Tongue and lip piercings can cause damage to your teeth and gums, as well as nerve damage, which can cause numbness and speech problems. See your dentist if you are thinking about having this done so that you are aware of all the risks before you make your decision.

Illegal drugs

Illegal drugs can cause tooth grinding, a dry mouth, tooth decay and gum disease. To help prevent this, maintain good teeth hygiene, don't rub drugs onto your gums, chew sugar-free gum, cut back on sugary drinks and foods and see your dentist regularly. Give up if you can (see page 132).

Oral sex

The Human Papilloma Virus (HPV) can lead to oral cancer in both men and woman, and it may be transmitted by oral sex as well as genital sex. Often there are no signs or symptoms, but if you do notice anything unusual in your mouth, go see your dentist. (Having said that, most people who are exposed to HPV do not develop cancer).

Dental Care

Here's how to keep your teeth sparkling till you are really, really old (like 40).

Avoiding problems

- Snack on savoury foods rather than sweet ones
- Drink lots of water, and make it tap (which has fluoride) rather than bottled, although if there is no other choice, bottled water is better than a soft drink
- Which brings us to: Avoid sugary drinks. Even sugar-free drinks contain a lot of tooth-eroding acid. If you can't avoid them, drink them through a straw and swish your mouth with water after you've finished them
- Chew sugar-free gum. It's obviously a better choice than sugary gum but is also good for your teeth because it increases protective saliva production and the chewing itself may decrease the risk of cavities
- See the dentist as frequently as every 6 months to a year – maybe more if you are a smoker or diabetic, maybe less if you are a good flosser. Going to the dentist is not covered by Medicare but you may get a rebate (part of your money back) from your health insurance, depending on what you chose to include in your plan when you took out your insurance.

Checklist: Cleaning your teeth

Make sure you are:

- Cleaning your teeth twice a day for two minutes with a fluoride toothpaste and a soft toothbrush
- Using a soft toothbrush, massaging the gums and cleaning the teeth with small circular motions
- Avoiding scrubbing horizontally and making sure you brush all surfaces of the teeth, including the inside
- Flossing to remove plaque and food debris every day (yes, really). Leaving your dental floss in the shower can be a good reminder
- Throwing away your toothbrush when it is looking shaggy, at least every 3 months.

Issues Relating To The Party Life

Socialising may or may not form a big part of your life at the moment, but it's worthwhile remembering a few things to keep you and your friends safe when you go out.

Checklist: How to party safely

Make sure you:

- Plan how you will get home at the start of the night, not the end
- Eat a full meal before you go out (including protein such as meat, cheese, eggs or dairy) – it slows the absorption of alcohol
- Stay with your friends and look out for each other
- Trust your own judgement – if it seems dodgy, it probably is
- Stay in a safe environment – streets with enough lighting and not too quiet
- If it looks like things are getting out of control or a fight is brewing, leave and go somewhere else
- Remember that you can have a great time without trashing yourself
- Drink water or soft drinks in between alcoholic drinks and try not to drink in a round or drinking game as you can end up drinking more than you want
- Don't drink and take drugs
- Know how much you are drinking – pour your own drinks and don't let others top you up
- Don't leave your drink lying around – it can be a target for spikers and result in sexual assault

- Don't sext – it's out of your control once you've sent it and could float round the Internet for years
- Don't experiment with new drugs while you're out – if it's something you really feel you have to do, make sure you are somewhere safe and with friends. Also remember that it's dangerous to use by yourself
- Don't drink and drive or let your friends do it
- Don't swim if you're drunk or have taken drugs
- Don't have unprotected sex – carry condoms
- Keep enough money as an emergency stash (and don't spend it at the bar)
- Don't walk home alone – have the number of someone you can call even if it's really late.

How to look after a drunk friend

This information is provided by Drug and Alcohol Research and Training Australia (DARTA)[37], with thanks to Paul Dillon.

You know that getting drunk can cause all sorts of problems to your health and to your security. But a hangover isn't the worst part – alcohol poisoning can also kill you. This happens in three ways: it can suppress the heart and breathing to the point where you stop breathing and your heart stops beating, you can become unconscious and choke on your own vomit, or it can react with other drugs or medications you have taken.

So, if you are in the position of looking after a drunk friend, please do the following:

- Stick with them and never leave them alone – not even to go to the toilet. They could lock the door and become unconscious, with you unable to get in
- Monitor them. The line between being drunk and being poisoned can be fine and if a person is already unwell and has drunk alcohol in the past hour or so, it could still be being absorbed and they will get worse. Stay there until they are feeling better
- Reassure them. When you are unwell after drinking it can be very frightening. It's important to have friends nearby
- Keep them comfortable. If they are feeling sick they may feel feverish so putting a cold compress (or even a cold water bottle) on the back of the person's neck can make them feel much more comfortable. Make sure that there is also something warm to wrap around them just in case they start to get cold
- Keep them hydrated. Hydration is a difficult one. If they are not being sick, make sure they replace lost fluids, i.e. if they have been urinating a lot, they need to drink water. For someone who is vomiting, soak a T-shirt or cloth in cold water and then have the person suck on that in between being

sick. That way, they are rehydrating and also making their mouth feel a little more pleasant, but not gulping down water that is likely to make them vomit more

• If in doubt, call for help. It is not an issue if, by the time the ambulance arrives, everything is okay. Also, it's important to know that the police will not attend a medical emergency involving alcohol or other drugs, unless another crime such as violence, has taken place.

Checklist: When to call an ambulance

How do you know if a person is just drunk or is suffering from alcohol poisoning? Seek emergency medical help if:

• The person is unconscious and can't be woken up by pinching, prodding or shouting

• The skin is cold, clammy, pale or bluish or purplish in colour, indicating that they're not getting enough oxygen

• The person is breathing very slowly. If there are more than 10 seconds between breaths, this is an emergency

• The person is vomiting without waking up.

Ambulance Costs

Medicare does not cover trips in an ambulance and these can be very expensive (up to $2000 for one trip). However, the good news is that you may already be covered by your private health insurance plan or if you are a full-time student, up to the age of 25, by your parents' plans, so check it out.

If you aren't covered, in some states (such as NSW), you can purchase cover through your health insurance, in others (such as Victoria) you need to join the Ambulance Organisation itself[38]. It isn't that expensive. For example, in 2014, the annual cost for Ambulance Membership in Victoria was just over $40.

But remember, whatever your cover, if you need an ambulance, call one.

Drugs

We're talking about illicit drugs here. If you do choose to use drugs, remember:

• Don't ever be coerced into drug taking. It's your body and you have the right to decide what goes into it

• Make sure that you don't use alone and that there is a non-drug taking friend to look after you. Tell them what you are going to take and tell them if you don't feel well

• Don't swim, and keep away from water or other potentially risky situations; don't use and drive

• Don't mix your drugs (and that includes taking alcohol and drugs together)

• Remember that drugs affect people differently so what might have suited your friend might not be good for you

- While you can never be sure, try to know what it is you are taking
- Don't use drugs by injection – it creates a whole different set of issues to consider
- Use a condom if you are having sex. Every time
- Don't ever be involved with drugs overseas. Other countries have different laws to ours and many have the death penalty for drug-related crimes.

In Australia, call 000 for ambulance and 112 if your mobile phone is out of range. For emergency services elsewhere dial 999 in the U.K., 911 in the U.S. and 112 in Europe.

Where can I get help with a drug or alcohol problem?

If you need help for yourself, a friend or a family member who has an alcohol or other drug problem, have a look at the following:

- If it's information you're after, go to the Australian Drug Foundation . You'll find lots of fact sheets, articles and web pages about different drugs as well as how to get help or referrals
- If it's help you need but you would rather just go on-line and not face-to-face, look at Counselling Online which provides free, 24/7 on-line counselling with professional counsellors. It's all done through your keyboard, not by phone or in person.

Five Top Tips

1. If someone at home or at work is sick, wash your hands frequently. It can stop you catching whatever they've got

2. Place a burn in cold water for 20 minutes and avoid using anything else such as Aloe Vera, butter or ice packs

3. If you are looking after a drunk friend stick with them and don't leave them alone – not even for them to go to the toilet

4. Replace a knocked-out tooth into your mouth after washing with milk or saliva, and see a dentist within 15-20 minutes. This gives you the best chance of saving it

5. If you think you might need an ambulance, just call one. Don't be concerned about the cost, whether one is really necessary or whether the police will become involved. Police are only concerned if a crime has taken place, whereas paramedics just want to keep you alive.

With many thanks to Dr Martine Burger and Dr Marianne Kagiaros
for their help in writing this chapter.

CHAPTER **8**

CLOTHING CARE 101

You know how at home the dirty clothes in the washing basket make it back into your cupboard and are sometimes even ironed? Sadly, that just doesn't happen when you move out. If you don't take action yourself, you'll end up looking like your little brother on a bad day. Or worse.

Haven't Got Time To Read The Whole Chapter? Read This.

1. There is a care label on all of your clothes that will tell you whether it can be machine washed, what temperature you should use and whether or not you can use the tumble dryer. Check it out to avoid washing disasters. If in doubt, wash in cold water

2. If you hang out clothes on the line carefully you can avoid a lot of ironing. Put shirts on hangers and for the rest, if it's a bottom hang it from the top (e.g. jeans get hung by the waistband), if it's a top hang it from the bottom (e.g. t-shirts get hung by the hem)

3. Shoes need care so clean them, polish them and have them re-soled or heeled as required. That way they'll last longer and look better

4. Different types of jewellery require different types of care. Gold should be soaked in warm water, silver should be cleaned with silver cleaner or using bicarb-soda and aluminium foil, pearls should be washed or wiped and diamonds are best done in a jewellery shop

5. Moths love stains on natural fabrics so make sure your woollens are put away clean. At the first sign of a moth or larvae, take action. Protect your clothes by washing them and then get serious with the moths.

Washing Your Clothes

There are four main ways of washing your clothes – in the machine, by hand, soaking (actually, I'm not sure this counts as washing) and dry cleaning. Don't dry clean your everyday clothes. Who knows what chemicals they use and you want to put them against your skin? You've got to be kidding. And not only that, it's really expensive. Of course, you may have to dry clean precious items such as winter coats, suits or evening wear, but don't make it a habit for your run-of-the-mill items.

Machine washing

Before you wash anything, always make sure you read the care label (which is different to the size or brand label) on the inside of your clothes. You'll find that most items can be machine washed especially jeans, shorts, t-shirts, hoodies, night wear, underwear and sports gear (but not compression wear if you want it to last).

Materials that are NOT good candidates for machine washing include silk, some wools, special finish items (e.g. anti-mosquito clothing), formal wear and clothes with a decorative finish (such as sequins).

Checklist: Machine washing

- Wash your coloured clothes and your whites separately to avoid greying the whites. The one exception to this is that you can wash light blue clothes with the whites. In fact, in the olden days, people used to add a 'blueing agent' to their whites – which bizarrely made them seem whiter. Be particularly careful not to wash anything red with your whites or you'll end up pink all over. Also be particularly diligent on the first few washes of new items when colours are most likely to run
- Use hot water for whites, and cold or warm water for colours. This will help keep your colours brighter for longer
- Wash black items inside out (to maintain their 'blackness') and avoid using detergents with optical whiteners as they cause black clothes to fade. Check out the side of the box
- Spray stain remover on cuffs and collars of shirts that are grubby before you add them to the machine. Wait a minute before you turn the machine on to allow the stain remover to act
- Use the right detergent for your machine (i.e. for a top-loader or a front-loader) and for the temperature of water you have chosen
- Look at the box and see how much detergent the manufacturer recommends. Halve it and you'll find that the clothes will generally still come out clean

- Make sure you add detergent before you add the clothes as this helps it dissolve, which means you don't get powdery marks on your clothes. Many top-loading machines have a specific place for detergents, often in the centre column. Placing the powder there will ensure the detergent dissolves
- If an item is stained, wash the stain as soon as possible. A soak in COLD water is a good thing. Hot water can make some stains permanent
- Use a net washing bag for items that you want to protect (such as small delicate items) or to avoid stretching (such as tights). Also, place underwire bras into a bag as a loose underwire in the washing machine's workings can mean an expensive call-out fee.

Hand washing

You'll need to hand wash some items, particularly ones that are made of wool or silk, or which are very delicate. Also, some sportswear prefers to be hand washed and if so, it will say so on the label. Personally, I find this a real bore but it can't be helped. Here's an effective way to do it.

- Dissolve hand washing liquid, Velvet Soap or shampoo (but definitely NOT washing powder) in warm water. Make sure the water isn't hot
- Immerse the clothes and gently swish around. No stretching, pulling or wringing
- Leave to soak for around five minutes
- Pull the plug out and drain. Rinse by refilling the sink with warm water and gently swishing the item around; pull the plug out and drain again. Gently squeeze the excess moisture out
- Lay the item on a towel on the floor, then roll up the towel
- Stand on it (yes, stand on it), stepping along the length of the towel. This dirties your towel but gets most of the water out of your precious item, which helps avoid any of the dangers associated with hanging the item up (in particular, stretching). If it's not too precious you can spin dry in the machine on a gentle setting instead
- Hang, well supported, on a drying rack or if it's not too sunny a day, across a couple of lines on the clothesline. Be careful as the sun can cause delicate items to fade. Woollens are best laid flat to dry to avoid stretching.

Soaking

Soaking is your friend when you are time poor and active (read: dirty). Camping gear and winter sports gear just love a good soak. Just fill your sink with warm water, add detergent (powder or liquid), MAKE SURE IT DISSOLVES and chuck the items in. If they are (were) white, you can use a soaker designed for the purpose, such as a nappy bleaching solution.

Avoid soaking different colours together as the colour may leach, or soaking items with metal trims which may leave rust stains if soaked for longer than an hour. Also make sure that you soak all of the item, not just the affected part, as you can end up with colour changes in the soaked area that will look rather strange once dry.

Soak from an hour to several days, then machine wash as usual.

Stain Removal

- In general, the quicker you get to a stain, the more successful you will be with its removal
- If there is some solid matter to the stain, (e.g. food, mud, blood), remove the excess with a blunt knife and then treat
- If in doubt, rinse in cold water until as much of the stain is removed as possible, then soak. If the stain is of a greasy nature, use warm water.

There are a few types of stain that require special treatment.

Stain	Treatment
Chewing gum	Freeze, then scrape off any excess and dab with Eucalyptus oil. Wash.
Ink	Be careful! Refer to a dry cleaner as soon as possible. Do not wash as this may spread and/or set the stain but if you are desperate, sponge with methylated spirits.
Lipstick	Dab with methylated spirits.
Mud and paint	Use hot water to clean. If the stain remains after washing, use a commercial stain remover.
Sunscreen	Dab with methylated spirits, then wash.
Wine	Pour on soda water then soak as usual.

Tumble Drying

Only tumble dry things you are sure can stand it – jeans, casual clothes, underwear, pyjamas and most sports gear. Some socks and t-shirts don't like it so if in doubt, hang them up to dry. Never wool! Never silk! Never the cat!

And if you don't want to burn your house down, clean out the lint from the tumble dryer every now and then (like every time actually).

Hanging Out Washing

People are idiosyncratic when it comes to hanging out their clothes. My grandmother would never have hung her 'smalls' (they didn't wear undies in those days) on the outside line, but would have carefully hidden them on the inside one. But there are two other reasons to hang out clothes properly – to decrease drying time, and to avoid creases which you may need to iron out later (Ugh! Avoid ironing at all cost.)

To save time I leave my pegs on the line, masses on one line for socks and undies, not so many on the next couple of lines for t-shirts, jeans, shirts etc. and then only a couple on the last line for sheets. With hanging out, the general rule is that you hang tops from the bottom (e.g. a t-shirt gets hung from its bottom hem) and bottoms from the top (e.g. a pair of jeans gets hung from the waistband).

Socks

Hang out socks in pairs from the tops, not the toes. When they're dry just fold them together as you take them off the line. Lay them flat on top of each other and fold them so they are around 10cm long – that usually means in half for short socks and in thirds for longer socks. Insert the thumbs of both your hands into the opening of one sock, then with your fingers of both hands turn that layer of the open end of the sock over all the other layers and inside out. You'll end up with a neat, flat little packet. Huh? Sounds confusing – but try it.

Business shirts

Hang business shirts on coat hangers on the line, with a peg on either side of each hook to stop them all sliding in to each other. This will minimise the amount of time you will need to spend ironing them. You can also hang other shirts and t-shirts in this manner as well, or peg them upside down by their hems at the sides. Both ways mean that you don't end up with marks at the shoulders that may be unsightly or difficult to iron out.

Jeans

Hang up jeans by the back waistbands at the side seams but only through one layer so the front falls open. Because jeans are so thick they take ages to dry but hanging them in this manner will help.

Underwear

Hang underwear by one side seam, hanging down. Hang bras by one side of the chest band.

Sheets

Hang sheets so that you end up having the top edge of the sheet along one line, and the bottom edge of the sheet along the next, with the bulk of the sheet draped down between the two lines. This minimises creases, and also means they dry more quickly than if you had hung them together from one line.

Hang the sheet directly out of the washing basket, pegging one end of the sheet along one line, pulling the basket along with you as you go. Then hang out the other side on the next line, again pulling the basket with you as you go. This means at no time do you have to carry the heavy wet sheet yourself or risk part of it scraping on the ground as you peg. When it's dry, you just fold it off the line.

Silk

Be careful hanging silk out in the sun – it fades very quickly and one day on the line in a scorcher can wreck your precious dress or silk shirt irreversibly. Better to hang it up inside.

Ironing

If you can possibly find a flat mate who likes ironing, then grab them with two hands and never let them go (but not in a weird way). Some people like ironing in front of TV, though for if you're like me, nothing can make ironing a pleasure. So, it's important to know how to do it properly to minimise the time required. Follow the steps below to make it easy. Well, easier.

Avoid ironing if you can

When you are clothes shopping, look for items that won't need ironing. Yay! If your clothes do need ironing, hang them out to dry neatly and carefully as detailed earlier in the chapter. Always fold laundry as soon as it comes off the line, and don't leave it jumbled in the laundry basket. Remove items promptly from the tumble dryer – hot, scrunched up clothes will lead to cold, really scrunched up clothes! And finally, if you are having a shower, try hanging the item you need to press in the bathroom with you without the fan on – the steam can make creases disappear

Preheat the iron

Always check you have the iron on the correct temperature for the item of clothing you are ironing. Yes! There are different settings on an iron ranging from synthetic (very cool) to linen (very hot). If you don't use the right setting for the right item of clothing, you could end up with a disaster – melting a synthetic top if the iron is too hot, or wasting your time and achieving nothing on linen if the iron is too cool.

Fill the iron with water and have it set on 'steam' if you are ironing very creased items of clothing, or those made from cotton or linen. Similarly, it can help to have a spray bottle of water handy to spray the item before you run the iron over it.

If possible have a very large ironing board. Ironing boards are amazingly expensive, and you may think it's a waste of money buying a large one when you plan not to be doing too much ironing at all! If you have the budget and the storage space, buy a big one, as it will minimise time spent ironing, which has to be a good thing

One last tip, if you cool or warm tumble dry an item when it is still slightly damp (not wet), it can minimise the ironing required. Excellent!

Business shirts

If you are a man, one skill you need to have is how to iron a man's business shirt. On the other hand, if you are a woman, one skill you must never acquire is how to iron one! If you do, there'll always be a man who'll ask you to do his ironing for him. And this is a very bad thing.

Here is one way in which you men can iron your shirts:

- Iron the collar, laying it out flat on the ironing board
- Now iron the outside (right side) of one cuff, unfolding it to do so, followed by the same sleeve, laying it flat on the ironing board to do so. Now do the other cuff and sleeve
- Iron one front yoke (the top of the front), then the back yoke, then the other front yoke
- Finally, iron the back then the two fronts. This means you iron the part you are most likely to see last so it does not run the risk of being crushed while you iron the rest of the shirt.

(And for you very clever cookies out there – yes, you iron a women's business shirt the same way!)

Trousers

Ironing trousers can be fiddly. The key here is to iron them laying them down on their side, so that you end up with a crease down the front and the back of each trouser leg. Lay them on the ironing board sideways, iron the inside of one leg and the outside of the other then flip them over and iron the inside of the other leg and the outside of the other. All done.

T-shirts

Okay, these are easy-peasy – just lay them flat with the front facing you and iron the sleeves first, followed by the body. If you are fussy or the fabric is thick, turn them over and iron the sleeves and body of the other side. But remember that t-shirts tend to look less creased as you wear them so some people never iron t-shirts at all.

You've got to be kidding

Never, ever bother to iron the following: jeans, sheets, tea towels or underwear (need I say more?).

Cleaning Shoes

Leather shoes

If you lash out on a really expensive pair of work shoes or fabulous boots, you want them to last, and one way to achieve that is to polish them regularly.

Again, there's no absolutely right way to do it but here's one method:

- Clean off any mud with a coarse brush that you keep for this purpose
- Apply shoe polish or Dubbin – which you can use on any colour leather and is cheaper than polish - smoothly with another coarse brush. Make sure it's not too thick but that you take particular care of the toes and heels (where a lot of scuffing occurs)
- Leave for a couple of minutes then brush off with a softer polishing brush
- Finally, buff with a soft cloth.

If your shoes are wet, stuff them with newspaper, and allow them to dry away from heat before you clean them. This will prevent the leather cracking.

For really good shoes keep an eye on the soles and in particular the heels. A cobbler will be able to replace them to get another few years of life out of your precious shoes. It can be expensive but worth it if you really like them.

Patent leather shoes

Clean with Vaseline (Petroleum Jelly) – yes, really!

Suede shoes

Don't get suede shoes wet – this will mark them irreversibly. Never use any sort of polish on them but instead brush them with a special suede brush bought from a shoe shop, or gently use steel wool. Suede shoes are not easy to clean so be careful with them and try not to wear them on a wet day. Alternatively, to prevent stains, you can buy a waterproofing spray for suede shoes although some people think this changes the look of the suede.

Muddy sports boots and hiking boots

With sports boots (such as those for footy, hockey, lacrosse etc.) or hiking boots, make sure you let them dry away from direct heat (such as a heater) as this can make the leather crack. Once dry, brush off the dried mud with a stiff brush. If they are still very dirty, use warm soapy water and a brush to clean them but try not to immerse them in the water. Then wipe them with a damp cloth and leave to dry.

Sports shoes

Most runners or sport shoes can be washed in warm soapy water, rinsed in clear warm water and then left with the tongues pulled open to dry. Let them dry in the air outside or hang them by their laces on the clothesline.

Cleaning Jewellery

Gold

To clean gold jewellery, soak it for 15 minutes in warm water with a splash of dishwashing liquid. Rinse with clear water. Because gold is a soft metal, be sure to store it away from other jewellery so that it doesn't get scratched.

Silver

Cleaning silver jewellery (and other silver items too) is an alchemist's dream! Silver cleaner works very well but why don't you try this? Bring a large non-stick or stainless steel pot of water to the boil. Add in several tablespoons of bi-carb soda and a large piece of scrunched up aluminium foil. Immerse your silver items in to the frothing mess and swirl around with a wooden spoon. Once they are clean (and this may take a bit more bi-carb soda), rinse them with warm fresh water and leave them to dry on a tea towel. Don't use an aluminium saucepan as you can end up with a black pan!

Pearls

Pearls are very delicate – they can scratch easily and because they are porous, they are vulnerable to hairspray and perfume. Wash them in warm water with dishwashing liquid added, rinse them and then let them dry on a soft towel. Try not to get them too wet as this can cause their thread to weaken and break. Store them in a soft pouch, and wear them often so that the oils in your skin improve their lustre. Apparently pearls don't like sweat, so if you've been wearing your pearls to do a spin class, give them a wipe before you put them away.

Diamonds and other stones

The best way to clean diamonds is by going to a jewellery shop and asking if they would please clean them in their ultrasonic cleaner (this works best if they know you or if you've actually bought something from the shop). Otherwise at home you can use warm water and detergent and a soft brush but be careful as you don't want to damage the setting. You can also use a dental irrigation device to remove dirt from the claws.

Clothes Maintenance

You'll need a few things in your sewing kit to do any quick running-repairs or to take up a hem every now and then.

Sewing on a button

It's not very cool to run back home to get a button sewn on and they only take a minute to do yourself, so it's a really useful skill to learn. Here you go.

First of all thread a sharp needle with a thread that is the length of about one and a half times the distance from your elbow to the tip of your finger. Pull the thread through the hole till one side is about twice the length of the other. Tie a knot in the end of the long thread, and hold the button onto the fabric with your finger on one side and your thumb on the other where you want it to be located.

Starting on the inside of the item, come up through the fabric and then through one of the holes of the button that you are holding in place. Pull the thread all the way through. Place a pin horizontally across the button and go down into the other hole, over the top of the pin and pull the thread all the way through. The reason you have a pin there is to give some slack to the thread as you are sewing on the button.

Then come up through the first hole again (or in the case of a four button hole, through the first of the other two holes) and down through the second (or fourth), repeating this about six times. Once you have done this, remove the pin, insert the needle from the top to below the button but not through the fabric (so the needle is now between the button and the item of clothing) and wrap the thread around the shank a couple of times. Then pass the needle back down through the fabric to the inside of the garment, tie a knot, then cut it off. Easy!

Pilling

Pilling is when those little balls of rubbed fabric suddenly appear on your jumper, particularly on woollen clothes and in areas of wear, such as along your sleeves or under your arms. The best way to remove this is by a little battery-operated clothing shaver designed for the purpose but beware! You can put a hole in a cashmere jumper by over-enthusiastic shaving.

Make sure you remove pilling, as it looks cheap and tacky.

Mending

Repairing a small tear

Remember that old saying 'A stitch in time saves nine'? Fix something early on before it has time to develop into a big problem. (And if it does, see *Repairing A Large Hole Using A Patch*, later on in this chapter).

Try to get to the hole before it's much larger than half a centimetre (¼ of an inch). Thread a sharp needle with a matching colour and type of thread. For instance, if it's a cotton item of clothing, use normal cotton thread. Over time try to collect a set of good quality threads from a sewing shop and don't use supermarket thread – it frays and breaks and can drive you crazy, not to mention leave you with another hole to fix again. If the item is woollen, use a thicker woollen thread designed for mending purposes. You can buy this at a sewing shop.

A hole on a seam

If the hole is on a seam, you are in luck! Turn the clothing inside out and sew along the seam line, doing back stitch. (This is a very easy yet sturdy stitch – have a look at Youtube and in two minutes you'll be backstitching like the best of them.) Or if that's not possible, just sew over the edge, enclosing the seam with each stitch. When you turn the clothing right side out again, you won't be able to see it. Easy.

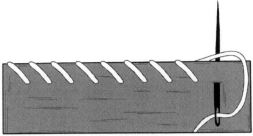

A hole in the middle of the fabric

If it's not at a seam (i.e. in the middle of the fabric), lay the fabric flat, or even better, stretch it VERY SLIGHTLY over a light bulb or a wooden darning mushroom (see illustration below).

Bring the needle up from underneath at the edge of the hole, then take the thread down through the middle of the hole and up through the edge of the fabric on the opposite side of the hole. Then go down through the hole again and come up through the fabric next to where you took your first stitch. If you pull a little bit tightly on each stitch, you'll end up with something that looks a bit like a spider, joining it all together. Take the thread through to the underside, tie a knot and cut it off.

Repairing a large hole using a patch

If it's a large hole you can't just pull it together with stitching as this will cause it to pucker. You will need to patch it. Cut a piece of fabric in a neat shape 1cm larger all around than the hole, any shape you like but most common is a square or a circle. Place it in the required place so that the hole is completely covered. Pin around the edges of the patch, making sure that you pin only the patch and the top layer together, and not the back of the garment as well.

Beg, borrow or steal a sewing machine, and sew as neatly as you can in a zigzag stitch around the edge of the patch. This can be tricky if it's on the leg of jeans, so you will have to slide the jeans on the arm of the machine and sew 2 sides, then take the jeans off, slide them on the other way and sew the next 2 sides.

If you really can't get a machine, then using double thread, or even better, embroidery thread, sew around the patch with diagonal stitches in one direction and when you get to the start again, sew back around the other way crossing each of the stitches. Take the thread down to the wrong side, tie a knot and cut off the excess thread.

Darning

Darning is a skill that is fast disappearing. I'm not sure that anyone expects you to darn your socks but trust me, it is very Zen and there is a strange satisfaction in darning, so here goes: put the sock on a light bulb or a darning mushroom and thread a darning needle with matching woollen thread. Sew some long stitches across the hole in parallel lines. Then turn the socks 90° and going above and below each of the parallel lines do another row of parallel lines at right angles to the first set. It's a bit like weaving. Once you have covered the hole, weave the end of the woollen thread through a part of undamaged sock for about 2cm and then cut off the excess thread.

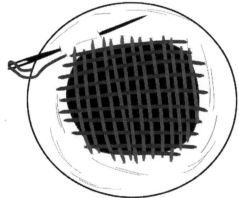

Taking Up Hems

Taking up trousers or a skirt by hand

Try on your trousers or skirt and get a friend to pin up a small part of the hem at approximately the right level. Have a look in the mirror and check that it's the right length. When you are happy with the length of the hem, remove your item of clothing and if it's a skirt slide it inside out on an ironing board; if it's a pair of jeans lay them flat, inside out, on a table. Measure the amount of hem you need to fold up. A hand sewn hem is usually larger than a machine sewn one – you will need around 4cm for the hem itself so if for instance the amount you need to fold up is 10 centimetres wide, you will need to cut off 6 cm. Very accurately cut off the required amount using a tape measure or ruler to guide you.

Using the iron, press 1cm of the hem under onto the wrong side. Next fold over another 3cm and press again (giving you the total of 4 cm) and put pins through all layers at the top folded edge of the hem.

Thread a sharp needle with a matching coloured thread and tie a knot in the end of the thread. Insert the needle into the fold of the hem – travel 1cm towards yourself then bring the needle out of the hem fold. Now, take a small stitch of the fabric. Insert the needle again. Insert the needle again into the fold of the hem, pass it another centimetre towards you and bring it out of the fold of the hem then take another small stitch of the fabric.

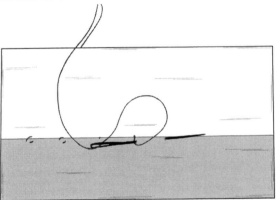

Continue in this manner until you have gone around the whole hem. The end result is a hem that is reasonably secure where you can only see tiny stitches on the outside of the garment. Tie the thread off securely.

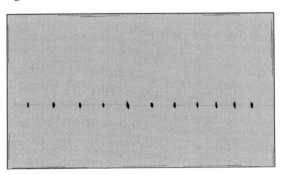

Taking up trousers or a skirt by machine

This is very similar to taking up trousers or a skirt by hand but as machine hems are smaller than hand-sewn hems you will need only 2½ centimetres for the hem itself. So if the fold up you have is 10cm you will need to cut off 7½ cm all around. Very accurately cut off the required amount using a tape measure or ruler.

Using the iron, press 1cm of the hem up onto the wrong side. Now press up the next 1½ cm and pin through all layers of fabric at the top folded edge of the hem.

Using a sewing machine and a straight stitch of medium length, sew through the hem all the way around on the inside. When you get to the start of the stitching again, do a few more stitches, then reverse for a few stitches. The end result will be a very strongly stitched hem with the stitches visible from the outside. This is an ideal hem to use for jeans.

Storing Your Clothes

Folding versus hanging

Always fold your jumpers rather than hanging them to avoid the stretching caused by coat-hangers. The contrary is true for business shirts; it is better to hang them to avoid the creases caused by folding them.

Shoe storage

Shoes can be smelly, and ones that you use regularly are much better left on a shoe rack to air than hidden away in a drawer. Good shoes, though, are happier in a shoebox as they are protected from rubbing against other shoes.

One thing to remember is that it's best if you can avoid wearing shoes two days in a row as they need to dry off between wears. This can be difficult to avoid, but it's better for your shoes if you can.

And Finally...Moths

Types of moths

Did you know there are two types of household moths? The first ones are those horrible ones that seem to appear from nowhere in your pantry – Indianmeal moth or Plodia interpunctella (such a great name!) to be exact[41]. The second ones are the ones that enjoy eating the favourite and generally most expensive items in your wardrobe. Clothing moths (or Tineola bisselliella, if you need to know) love natural fabrics, in particular wool and cashmere, and even better if they have had human sweat, food or liquids dropped on them.

The eggs and larvae are tiny and very difficult to see. Often the first evidence of a moth invasion is when you find the white fluffy cocoons they leave behind. That is, until you hold up your favourite item and it is littered with holes and looks like lace. What a disaster!

How do you get rid of larvae and eggs?

Moths are not interested in clothes that are washed regularly or in frequent use. But if you are going to put away clothes for a couple of months, make sure they are very clean.

You can do any of the following to kill the eggs and larvae:

- Dry clean your clothes
- Wash them in water which is 60 degrees or hotter (but be careful with woollens as they can shrink)
- Put your clothes in a plastic bag in the freezer for several days, or
- Put them in a plastic bag in the hot sun for several hours.

It is unlikely that moths will be hanging out in any synthetic clothes or any of your more sturdy work or weekend wear, so concentrate on the natural fibres in your wardrobe.

How do you get rid of adult moths?

So, clean your clothes, and once you have the larvae under control, you can now attack the adult moths so they are no longer able to breed. The best way is to use hormone traps – they have a pheromone lure that attracts the male moth. Once all the male moths are stuck to the sticky trap the poor females die from broken hearts and there are no more baby moths. Cool. These traps are easily available at the supermarket.

You may also need to use a Pyrethroid surface spray on all surfaces of your wardrobe. Do not spray this directly on to your clothes. These chemicals can be toxic to cats and fish, and are not great for humans either, so use them in moderation.

Finally, when you are not wearing your woollens for some time, make sure they are clean and then store them in their own plastic bags in your wardrobe.

What shouldn't you use?

Old-fashioned mothballs are toxic if ingested by children or pets, they produce a gas that is carcinogenic and they are flammable. There is nothing good to say about mothballs (apart from the fact they can come in pretty colours) and they should be avoided.

Camphor wood chests have been used for centuries to help keep moth infestations at bay but although they smell great, it is doubtful whether the camphor-wood vapour builds up to the point where it can kill the larvae. The value of these chests lies more in the fact that they are well sealed and the moths can't access the clothes[42].

Five Top Tips

1. Don't machine wash silk, most wools, formal wear and clothes with a decorative finish

2. The quicker you get to a stain, the easier it is to remove. Always choose cold water for soaking unless it's mud or paint in which case use hot

3. To keep the tumble dryer working effectively, clean out its lint every time you use it. This will also help it to not catch on fire!

4. Make sure you set your iron to the right temperature for the type of fabric you are ironing. For instance, linen needs a hot iron; synthetics need a cool one

5. Clean patent leather shoes with Vaseline and suede shoes with steel wool.

CHAPTER 9

MY HOUSE IS A PIGSTY

Got a flat-mate who loves cleaning? A mother who wants to tidy up your new house? Or a genie in a bottle? Damn. It's going to be up to you then.

Haven't Got Time To Read The Whole Chapter? Read This.

1. Do a little bit of cleaning every day (just a little bit) and a bigger clean every week. Don't leave it till your place is filthy or till someone special is coming to visit as by then it will be a Herculean task

2. Start sweeping, vacuuming or mopping from the furthest corner of the room, working backwards to the door. Otherwise you'll need to walk over your clean floor when you've finished

3. Always wipe up a spill as soon as you see it. Fridges, ovens and microwaves can be really hard to clean once a stain sets. And on that note, wipe your oven door and base after every time you use it

4. Dry stainless steel as soon as you've wiped it – any water left will leave a mark

5. To get white rings off a wooden table use one of the following: petroleum jelly, olive oil & vinegar, mayonnaise & ash mixed together (yes, really!) or 'Brasso' brass cleaner.

A Cleaning Plan

If you stay on top of cleaning you won't find any nasty surprises. (What is that thing growing in the corner by the way?)

Every day

Don't panic, it's really only maintenance – not cleaning – and will only take a few minutes! Clean up any spills in the kitchen or on the bench tops as soon as they happen, otherwise they can become really tricky to get rid of later. Letting it cool a bit first (obviously), take 30 seconds to wipe out the oven every time you use it, otherwise spills get baked on and you'll need a nuclear blast to clean them up. Wipe up any mess in the microwave for the same reason. Sweep the floor when you can see that it is dusty or dirty. Do a two-second tidy up of each room as you leave it. Clean the toilet if there's a stain (see page 157). Finally, attend to any stains on carpets or upholstery immediately.

Every week

Do the dusting, remove cobwebs, clean toilets and basins, wipe mirrors, and mop and vacuum every week. Wipe out the microwave and oven, wipe the benches and clean the kitchen sink. Change the sheets on your bed every week, or at a stretch, every fortnight. And open some windows to give your place a good airing.

Every month

Clean out the fridge and throw away that jar of unidentifiable gunk that seems to be moving around the top shelf. Clean out the filter on the dishwasher (if you are unsure how to do this, find the instruction manual of your dishwasher on-line). Cleaning the filter takes about two minutes and ensures the dishwasher works effectively as well as stopping it from smelling. While you're there, put the filters of the exhaust fan over the stove through the dishwasher. Wipe over leather upholstery with a slightly damp cloth, dust the skirting boards and polish any wooden furniture. Sort out one shelf per month of your pantry or food cupboard, discarding out-of-date food and wiping down the shelf.

Every year

Wash your windows. Get the carpets cleaned professionally.

Products You Need

Not many people like cleaning, so make it easier by having the right tools. You don't need to spend a fortune on cleaning equipment but if it floats your boat and you can afford it, go for it! At a minimum you will need:

Hardware

- Broom
- Vacuum cleaner (essential if you have carpet, although can be useful for a wooden floor, too)
- Mop
- Mop bucket with wringer (get one on wheels and you will thank me every time you use it)
- Toilet brush and stand, one per toilet
- Rubber gloves for the kitchen and one pair that you leave near each toilet
- Cloths and sponges, including some micro-fibre cloths. Have separate ones for the kitchen, for general cleaning, and for toilets
- Cobweb brush, or at a stretch you can try to use the broom
- A squeegee for cleaning windows and the shower screen, or you can use scrunched up newspaper.

Cleaning products

- Toilet cleaner (make sure the bottle shape means you can spray under the rim of the toilet)
- Washing-up liquid for the dishes
- Floor cleaner (check that it's suitable for your type of floor)
- Window cleaner (or you can use water with a splash of vinegar)
- Spray cleaner for benches, such as an orange spray
- Liquid cleaner (such as a thick white cream) for harder to remove stains
- Furniture polish if you have wooden furniture
- Cleaner for the shower screen.

Dusting, Wet Or Dry

You should always work from top to bottom, so this means attacking dusting, cobwebs and mirrors before you do the vacuuming and/or the mopping.

Start your cleaning session with the dusting as this means the dust you disturb will settle on the floor, ready to be mopped or vacuumed up. You can use either a duster (often a fluffy little number) or a dusting cloth, but if you find the dust upsets the allergies of someone in your household, you can always wet-dust, using a slightly damp cloth and wiping over any surfaces. Or if you are the one who's allergic to the dust, tell your flat-mate you can't do it because of your health. Same with the vacuuming.

Dust or wipe all surfaces where dust may have settled such as mantelpieces, benches, tables, venetian blinds, windowsills and the tops of picture frames. For cobwebs, attack with a cobweb brush – it looks a bit like a big, flat toilet brush on a very long extendable handle. You can use a broom but it's likely to leave dirty marks on the wall and won't reach as high as the cobweb brush.

Sweeping & Vacuuming

Hard surfaces

Make sure you sweep or vacuum your floors well before mopping. Start in the corner furthest from the door, and then work backwards towards it. You should put your vacuum cleaner on the correct setting for a hard floor – often there will be a little etched drawing on the top of the head to show you which setting is correct. If it's not on the correct setting, it can be very difficult to move along the floor and may scratch some floor surfaces. Be thorough as any dust or grit left can scratch the floor, or leave streaks once you mop.

Carpets

Again, vacuum from a corner of the room, backwards towards the door. Make sure you keep an eye on the dust container of your vacuum cleaner and empty it as required. If the suction disappears, a full vacuum is the likely problem. Or else you've sucked up the cat.

Mopping

Mop from the furthest corner of the room, back towards the door. Keep your mop in contact with the floor, going backwards and forwards in large strokes, and clean it regularly in the bucket that you bring along with you. Make sure you wring out the mop firmly before you mop, keeping the mop damp but not soaking wet. This is particularly important for wooden floors, which can warp, stain or end up streaky if too much water is applied.

Excellent cleaning products are available at the supermarket for every type of floor. These need to be diluted into your mopping bucket according to the instructions on the bottle. Alternatively, you can make your own floor cleaners at home.

- For wooden floors, use warm water alone, or warm water with a splash of olive oil. Do not use hot water as this can cause the floor to crack
- For linoleum or tiles, use a small amount of detergent diluted in warm water

- For tiles or stone you can use warm water with a splash of vinegar added.

If you can, open the windows to help the floor dry and, to keep it clean, tell your idiot flat-mate not to walk on it till it is dry.

Bathroom

Toilet

If you use the toilet and there is a stain there after flushing (yep, I'm talking about poo here), use the brush to get rid of it, then flush again, holding the brush under the flushing water. If you don't do this, it can set hard and then be harder to remove later, particularly if it's high up on the bowl and not reached by the flushing water.

If you don't like the idea of poo on the brush, put a piece of toilet paper on the stain, then use the brush to rub it off. The toilet paper can then be flushed down the toilet. You will still need to run the brush under the flushing water to get all the paper off it. If you attend to stains as they occur, your weekly clean will be much easier.

For the weekly clean, you need to have a sponge and a pair of rubber gloves that are only used for this purpose – hang them on the u-bend behind the toilet, or in a plastic container marked 'toilet cleaning' in the cabinet under the bathroom basin.

Using the toilet cleaner, squirt liquid under the rim all around the bowl so that it drips down the inside of the toilet. This works best if the bowl is dry, so don't do it just after you've used the toilet. I like to use enough cleaner so that I almost cover the inside of the bowl with the drips. Leave it for at least five minutes.

Using the toilet brush, dip the brush into the water and scrub away the liquid, dipping into the water and scrubbing below the water line. Scrub all of the bowl, including under the rim. Finally flush the toilet and hold the toilet brush under the spray. Put it back into the holder. Now wearing your gloves, use the sponge to wipe over the seat, both on top and underneath. You can put some toilet cleaner on the sponge if you like, spray it with some spray cleaner, or just use it as is. There are also disposable toilet-cleaning wipes available which are flushable, although they are expensive and don't necessarily do a better job than cleaning with a sponge.

Rinse the sponge in the water in the toilet. You do know that this water is cleaner than some water you drink, don't you? You may find this hard to believe but in a study in Britain, the ice served in six out of ten chain restaurants had more bacteria than the water in their toilets[43].

If you can't bear rinsing the sponge in the toilet, use the sink.

Wring the sponge out and store with the gloves behind the toilet or under the basin.

Bathroom basin

Basins get grimy from soap residue and toothpaste, so make sure you clean them every week at least. Use a spray or liquid cleaner on a sponge, keeping this sponge only for use on the sink. Once you have wiped over the whole sink, rinse out the sponge and wipe over it again, removing all traces of the cream or spray. Finally, dry the basin with a tea towel that will then go into the wash.

Bath & shower recess

Baths and showers should be wiped over once a week as well. If you want to be green, you can use a micro-fibre cloth designed for the purpose. You could also use bi-carb soda and vinegar but the smell will put you off fish and chips forever! Alternatively you can just use shower spray and be done with it.

If you have mould problems, you can use a couple of drops of clove oil in a litre of warm water and use it to wipe down the problem areas. Clove oil kills mould. There are also commercial mould killer products available.

Bedroom

Changing your sheets

People have different ideas about this, but while the general rule has always been every week, you can probably get away with changing your sheets every second week if you're not a real grub. It can make things easier if you use two sheets and sleep between them, with the doona on top. This means that you only need to wash your doona cover every month or so as it is not in contact with your body.

Hospital corners

If your bottom sheet is not a fitted one, it is worth your while to learn how to do a hospital corner. This means the sheet will stay tucked in. Okay – I'm going to describe this in words, but it might be easier to get on to YouTube and watch a video. Hospital corners are as easy as pie to do, but hard to describe! First tuck in the sheet at the end of the bed. Then at each side, pick up the edge of the sheet at right angles to the end and fold it up so that it rests on the top of the bed. Tuck in the excess material down the side of the bed. Now fold the piece from the top of the bed down and tuck in. Some people will be impressed if you can do a hospital corner. Just one more thing you're good at!

Kitchen

Stove top

Always wipe down the stovetop as soon as you've spilt something. The heat from the stove bakes it on and it's a pain to remove later. If you haven't listened to this advice, then put a dripping wet cloth on the blob while you do something else for a few minutes. You should then be able to wipe it up easily but if not, then try again. If you're in the mood for some extra cleaning, you can take off any removable parts around the burners and soak them in hot soapy water.

Oven

I've said earlier that you should wipe out the oven every time you use it. Okay, so you've forgotten a few (like 20) times, and now it's filthy. There are industrial strength cleaners you can buy at the supermarket but these are pretty toxic, which doesn't seem a great idea to me for an appliance that cooks my food. Alternatively, you can call a company that will come and clean your oven while separating you from an enormous amount of money.

> ### CASE STUDY: OVEN CLEANING
> Russell moved into a new flat with his mates. His parents had taught him well about cooking a roast and he loved to whack one in the oven on a Sunday night for his friends. He hated cleaning his oven and didn't do it.
>
> After three years (and 150 roasts) the time came to move out of the flat and he found that the oven was so bad that he had to get it professionally cleaned before he could get his bond back. It cost $170 he couldn't afford.
>
> *Lesson: Wipe out your oven each time you use it*

If paying someone to clean your oven isn't in your budget, you can search on-line for an environmentally friendly method. Often these use a paste of bi-carb soda and water that you apply, leave on overnight, and then remove with a wet cloth. Next spray with vinegar and the remnants of the bi-carb soda go bananas with bubbling, just like those volcanos you used to make in school. A razor blade scraper can be great for really hard to remove grime. This method is said to work, but I would still highly recommend the 'thirty seconds each time' method of wiping it out every time you've used it. Make sure you wait till it cools down a bit first.

Extractor fan

Take off the filters and put them through the dishwasher – they will come out like new! Wipe the outside of the hood – wow, it's grubby!

Microwave

What? It's dirty? OK, so you're not perfect and you weren't wiping it out every time you used it. Now it's vile so wash the turntable with hot soapy water or put it in the dishwasher, and wipe out the inside of the microwave with a damp cloth. Don't forget the ceiling of the microwave; you may have to bend down to see it.

Sink

Sinks can get pretty mucky, so wring out a micro-fibre cloth in hot soapy water, making sure it's almost dry. Wipe over all the surfaces, and keep washing and wringing out the cloth to keep it clean as you wipe. Dry it with a tea-towel to make it look really spiffy. You can get stainless steel cleaners, but I'm not sure they're worth it for a sink. See Stainless Steel just below on this page.

Pantry

If you've been putting all your open food into containers, you shouldn't have a moth problem. Choose a shelf, and take out all the food. Wipe over the shelves, throw away any out-of-date food and wipe any containers that need it. Do a different shelf every month and you'll keep on top of it.

Other Cleaning Issues

Stainless steel

Stainless steel looks oh so stylish! But it can be a pain to keep clean, with fingerprints causing a particular problem. To clean it, you can use a micro-fibre cloth with plain water, and make sure you dry it well as watery spots can leave more marks. If this is not working well for you, you can buy a very effective stainless steel spray, or you can also use glass cleaner, or ammonia in water (the latter works well for glass as well). Make sure you rinse the surface you are cleaning after you use these products, then dry with a tea towel.

Wooden furniture

For modern wooden furniture, make sure that you keep it well dusted and look after it while you use it. Don't put items on that will scratch (or if you do, use a drinks coaster underneath), put a saucer under plants that could leak and try to keep the item out of the sun as this will cause fading. Never leave wet towels or clothing on wooden furniture as they will leave a water mark. And if you spill something on the table during dinner, always mop it up quickly.

To clean wooden furniture, use a good quality wood polish, rub it in with a clean soft cloth, and then buff with another soft cloth. Make sure you follow the manufacturer's instructions and don't use too much as it can leave a greasy finish which will attract dust. Sprays give a good result but can end up leaving a layer that can be hard to remove once it builds up.

Some furniture will have had a special finish applied, which means they will only require a quick wipe with a damp cloth and any oil that you put on will just serve to make them greasy. To check whether your furniture has this finish, you can just apply a small amount of polish on an inconspicuous area and see what happens. If it is absorbed, it's OK to use the polish. If it beads (like water on the sink), the furniture will just need a wipe with slightly damp cloth and a dry with a tea towel.

For antique wooden furniture, my advice is to be very careful! Buy a polish specifically for antiques, preferably one with beeswax and use it sparingly, buffing well to remove it.

To remove white rings from glasses on wood, there are several different methods:

- Rub petroleum jelly into the stain, leave overnight, and rub off
- Use olive oil and vinegar mixed together to rub off the stain
- Continuing in the salad theme, you can use mayonnaise mixed with a little ash to rub off the mark
- Or strangely, use 'Brasso' metal polish and rub from the outside of the stain to the inside.

Window cleaning

If you can, avoid cleaning windows on really hot days – the glass dries too quickly and it may streak.

Firstly, vacuum around the window frames (inside) and brush with a dry brush (outside), then wipe the frames both inside and out with a damp soapy cloth. To clean the glass, commercial window cleaning sprays are very effective but not always necessary. If the windows are very dirty, first clean them with warm, soapy water and a soft brush. Then use glass cleaning spray or clean water with a splash of vinegar, ammonia or methylated spirits added. A squeegee will remove all the water and prevent streaking of the glass as it dries, as will a ball of plain newspaper scrunched up and rubbed over the glass to dry it.

Venetian blinds

These are tricky little buggers to clean, but if you put socks over your hands and run them between the blades, it can work miracles! If they are in a really bad state, unclip them and take them out on to the grass, where you can scrub with hot soapy water then hose off. Good for the grass, good for the blinds!

Five Top Tips

1. Buy yourself a mop bucket on wheels. It may be low on your list of priorities but it will make mopping a joy (almost)

2. Start your cleaning up high with dusting, cobwebs and mirrors, and work your way down low to vacuuming and mopping

3. Clove oil kills mould. Add a few drops to a litre of water and wipe anything that is looking a bit dodgy

4. Anything wet left on wood will leave a white mark. If you do leave something on wood, take it off immediately and dry the wood with a tea towel

5. Don't clean windows on a hot day. They'll end up streaky.

CHAPTER 10

THAT'S MY CAR!

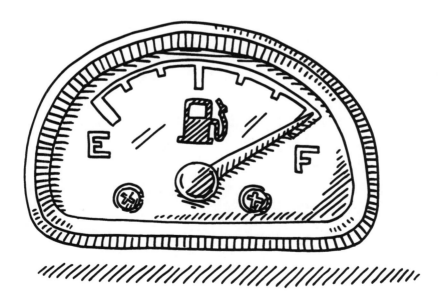

You're moving out – you've got the job, you've got the house and now it's time to get the car! There are a few things you need to know...

Haven't Got Time To Read The Whole Chapter? Read This.

1. The safest cars have side-curtain air bags, Electronic Stability Control (ESC), Anti-lock Braking System (ABS) brakes and seatbelt pre-tensioners

2. White is the safest car colour – it is involved in fewer accidents and if you do have an accident, is associated with a less severe outcome

3. To purchase your car, save as much as possible and borrow as little as possible, look for a low interest rate and pay back the loan as quickly as you can

4. While it's more expensive, there are benefits to insuring your car in your own name – there'll be no doubt you will be covered if you have an accident and with luck you will start to build up a no-claims history

5. While parking infringements don't give you demerit points, speeding fines do. If you get too many, you'll lose your licence.

Budgeting For Your Car

Apart from your house, your car is likely to be the biggest asset you'll buy. Cars are expensive! You will need to do your sums to work out how much that groovy little vehicle will actually cost you to buy and then to run.

Checklist: how much does a car cost?

In planning your car budget, you'll need to add in the cost of the following items:

- Purchase price of the car, or repayments for your car loan
- Insurance premium
- Registration
- Petrol
- Servicing
- And repairs, if you need them.

A car operating cost calculator (such as the one on the NRMA website[44]) can be a useful tool – just enter in the make and model of car, its cost and the insurance premium and the calculator will give you the weekly cost of running it. For example, a Mazda 3 which costs $24,490 to buy will cost around $189.69 per week or 66 cents per kilometre. If you have squirrelled away all the money to buy the car and don't need to take a loan, this reduces to $64.88 a week, or 22 cents per kilometre. An older car you pay cash for will cost you even less – a 2011 Mazda 3 will be down to 16 cents per kilometre. The lesson? Save up before you buy, and then buy second-hand.

Buying Your Car

Safety

Think carefully about the type of car you buy, particularly in terms of safety. There is a world-wide system rating new cars on their safety. In Australia, it is called ANCAP, in the U.S. it is NHTSA/IIHS and in Europe it is Euro NCAP. 1-star is the worst rating and 5-stars are the best. You are twice as likely to be killed or seriously injured in a 1-star rated car as a 5-star rated car[45].

According to the World Health Organisation[46], worldwide car accidents are the highest cause of premature death for 15-29 year olds worldwide. If your budget allows it, always try to buy a car with side curtain airbags, Electronic Stability Control (ESC), seatbelt pre-tensioners and Anti-lock Braking System (ABS) brakes[47]. It's worthwhile referring to the How Safe Is Your Car website[48] to check out the safety of cars you might be considering.

Colour

According to Monash University[49] white is the safest colour in terms of crash risk, particularly during daytime. They also say that if a crash does occur, there's the likelihood you'll be less injured in a white car than in any other colour car. One other thing to remember about the colour of your car: red fades more than other colours. So, if you do buy a red car, particularly an older one, make sure you wax it regularly to provide a protective layer.

Size

Buy a small car with a small engine, locally made or assembled (or at least not European) and don't modify it. Insurance companies believe these types of cars have fewer accidents and so they charge the cheapest insurance premiums for them.

Checklist: What is the safest car?

- ANCAP: 5 stars
- Colour: white
- Size: small
- Country of origin: local, or at least not European
- Features: side curtain air bags, ABS and ESC

Age

You'll need to think about the age of the car you want to buy. There are some excellent second-hand cars around and they are obviously much cheaper than new ones, so it pays to do your homework. Check how your potential purchase ranks in safety and of course get it checked by your local motoring organisation, but don't discount it just because it's old and not very cool.

Fuel

In general, there are three types of fuel available for cars. Most cars use petrol, but it is worth thinking about whether you might like an LPG or diesel-fuelled car instead. Whatever you decide, one thing to remember is never to put the wrong fuel into your car, such as petrol into a diesel car – you can totally stuff up the engine.

Which fuel will your ideal car use?

	Advantages	Disadvantages
Petrol	Widely available fuel Large choice of cars	Expensive fuel
Diesel	Better fuel economy Cars can have more torque (pulling power)	Dirtier emissions, but as more efficient can emit less CO_2 Cars are more expensive Cars are heavier so can have a less smooth ride Cars can cost more to repair, in particular fuel injectors & pumps
Liquid Petroleum Gas (LPG)	Inexpensive fuel – about 55% of the price of petrol[50]	Fewer choice of cars available Higher purchase price Car has less power Gas takes up space in the boot Cylinders need to be tested every 10 years so check the expiry date on the cylinder before you buy[51]

Paying For Your Car

Make sure you have thought about how you will finance your car before you go looking for it. Ideally you will have been saving dutifully – clearly it's best if you wait until you can pay cash and then buy what you can afford without a loan. If you haven't got cash, you need to do some serious planning now.

Be very careful about taking a loan from the car dealer. It is extremely tricky to work out what the final cost will be even if you are assured there is 'zero interest'. This interest rate may be for a limited time and then the interest rate reverts to one that is very high. There are also other charges that may be added. Car dealers bank on you being carried away with the delight of a quick purchase – and sign you up to a loan that may have significant drawbacks. Do your due diligence. Get on to a car loan comparison website[52] to get the best deal.

And have you explored other options, like your ever-loving family? Perhaps they may be prepared to loan you at least part of the money. To maintain harmonious familial relations you need to establish a pay-back schedule and stick to it.

How To Buy A Car

Visit some websites

The *CarSales* website is a good place to start as it will give you prices for both new and used cars from dealers and for cars being sold privately. You will already know new cars lose value very quickly once they leave the dealership, so if you want more bang for your buck, you'd be better buying a second-hand car and buying it privately. Privately sold cars are cheaper than those from dealers and besides you know car salesmen in car yards are notoriously dodgy.

Many second-hand cars are under warranty till they are five years old – check out the manufacturers' websites as warranty periods differ from car company to car company. But it's worth noting here that while the manufacturer's warranty passes on to the next owner, if the person selling the car has purchased an extended warranty it does not pass on to you.

A great option is to buy a known car from a family friend because they are likely to be more honest with you about the history of the car. If someone has the type of car you are after ask if they are planning to upgrade or sell – you never know unless you ask.

Test drive some cars

First of all, be prepared to look at lots of cars till you find the right one. When you do find a car that you are keen on, organise a test drive. If you can, drive on a variety of roads including local suburban streets and freeways to test the car at various speeds, and both during the day and at night. Bring a friend along who might notice something that you do not (and even better if they are a car enthusiast).

Negotiate the price

If you are happy with the car, negotiate the price. In the case of a private sale, make sure that the seller understands that you will only proceed if there is a satisfactory vehicle check. You should offer a significant discount to the asking price – say 20% – and with any luck you may end up with a 10% discount, particularly with a privately sold car. Stand your ground – remember there are lots of cars out there and they are just as keen to sell as you are to buy!

Check the history of the car

You'll want to know a bit about the history of the car, and in particular whether it has been written off after a severe crash, stolen, or if it has money owing against it. The first means that it could be dodgy mechanically; the other two mean that it could be taken away from you even if you've paid for it.

By using the Vehicle Identification Number or VIN (found on the inside of the car door, on the registration papers or on the engine, and which should all match) you can pay for a search to be done of a number of national databases which will give you this information. At the time of writing the most prominent companies were charging around $30 but with a bit of Internet trawling you can get a report for less than $10. Just type 'VIN check' into your Internet search engine.

Cooling off period

A cooling off period allows you to cancel the contract of sale if you change your mind. There is no cooling-off period on private sales[53]. With new car sales from dealers, there are different cooling off periods depending on where you live. In Australia for instance, Victoria gives you three business days to change your mind about buying a new car, in NSW it's one day and in Queensland it's none. Check what applies in your state.

Attend to the nitty gritty

Once the price has been agreed, get the car checked out by a mechanic. Many organisations offer this service but a good place to start is your local motoring association (search your state and 'motoring organisation'). If you are buying from a dealer you can skip this step, as they will offer you a warranty.

Read up on the details of *How To Register Your Car* below and print off the forms, or check that the vendor will be bringing them along. On the day of the transaction, organise a cover note for insurance (see page 171) and make sure that the paperwork is complete, then pay your money. Do not pay until the required paperwork has been completed and make sure you get a receipt for the money you have paid.

And don't forget to join your local motoring organisation. There is a waiting period after you join before you can use roadside assist (between one and seven days) so join up before you need it. (Some organisations will let you join on the spot when you have a problem, but you will pay a hefty fee for it. Check out whether this is available before you decide).

How To Register Your Car

If you buy from a dealer, the car registration will be handled for you.

If you buy from a private seller, you will need to change the registration from the seller's name to yours. Car registration is compulsory; the fee is paid to the government, and in most states of Australia includes Third Party Personal insurance (covering you for injury that your car causes to other people).

Because car registration is handled by State Governments, there are variations depending on where you are based. In some states, such as Victoria, the car will need a Road Worthy Certificate (RWC) before the registration is transferred, which is obtained by the seller from a mechanic. In NSW the vendor must have a 'green slip', which is proof of compulsory 3rd party insurance (CTP) before they can register a car.

To find out the procedure in your state, you'll need to look at the right websites – unfortunately it's a different organisation type in each state that handles the process.[54]

Car Insurance

Make sure you insure your car from the moment you first take possession of it. You can organise a cover note (temporary insurance) from your insurance company over the phone or the Internet.

How to insure your car

Things you will need to know to take out insurance include:

- The make of your car (e.g. Toyota)
- The model (e.g. Corolla)
- The year of manufacture of the car
- Whether there are any added extras (e.g. tow bars, anti-theft devices etc.)
- Whether you want to insure the car for replacement cost (i.e. for the amount it costs to replace the car at the time you have the accident) or for an agreed value (for example, the amount for which you bought the car).

Insure in whose name?

Think about whether you will have the car insured in your name or in a parent's name.

If it is in your name, insurance will be more expensive because younger drivers have more accidents. However, at the same time you will begin to build up your no-claim bonus rating while you have a relatively cheap car (cheap cars are cheaper to insure), rather than waiting to build it up when you have a more expensive one. Five years of no claims can decrease your premiums by a huge amount – up to 50-60%. If the insurance is in your name, you will also be sure that your car will be covered while you are driving, whatever the circumstances.

If your parents insure your car, the insurance will be cheaper. However, if your parents don't tell the insurance company you are the main driver of the car, you may not be covered in the case of an accident. You will also not be building up your no-claim history if your parents are insuring the car.

Decide what type of insurance you want

There are different levels of car insurance you can take out and these include (in order from cheapest to most expensive):

1. Third Party Personal – insurance which covers costs relating to an injury that your car causes to another person e.g. if you run over your neighbour and you break their leg. This is included in your registration cost

2. Third Party Property – this is insurance which covers damage to other cars or property by your car e.g. the damage caused if your car runs into your neighbour's fence and destroys it

3. Third Party Property, Fire & Theft – this covers damage to other property and cars as well as damage caused by fire and/or theft

4. Comprehensive – this covers everything outlined above as well as damage to your own car.

You will also need to decide if you want to add extras on such as windscreen replacement and roadside assistance – which come at a cost of course!

Decide what excess you want

An excess is the part of every claim that you yourself must pay before the insurance company kicks in the rest. Yes, this sounds counter-intuitive but it is the one way insurance companies have of avoiding frivolous claims. You can decrease your premiums (the amount you pay each year for insurance) by increasing the excess, so for instance you may get a 20% discount on the premium by increasing your excess from $600 to $1100. In this case it means that it is not worth your while to make a claim for anything worth less than $1100.

CASE STUDY: INSURANCE EXCESSES

Back to our friends Grace and Emily, who are now looking to insure their cars. Emily wishes to have a low excess of $600 and pays $1272 per year for her insurance, while Grace prefers to pay less for her insurance, so has increased her excess to $1,100. This means that her annual payment is $1022.

Sadly, they are both involved in an accident that causes $1000 damage to the bumper bar.

Emily makes a claim on her insurance, pays her excess of $600, and the insurance company pays the balance of $400. Grace does not make a claim, as she would need to pay the insurance company $1,100 (her excess) and as this is more than the cost of the repair, she organises and pays for the repair herself.

Lesson: there's no such thing as a free lunch. You pay less in premiums now, you'll pay more when you make a claim and vice versa

---

Compare premiums

It is easy to take out insurance on-line and it is worth getting on to a comparison website[55] to find the cheapest insurance available. There will be a wide range of prices for similar insurance. This is because some companies actively discourage younger drivers, while some companies are prepared to accept them as part of their overall insurance portfolio. It is therefore worth shopping around for the insurer that fits your particular needs.

What To Do If You Have An Accident

Look after people first

Immediately check that all passengers are okay. If not, call 000 (or 911 in the U.S., 999 in the U.K. and 112 in Europe). You will be asked whether you want Police, Fire or Ambulance and clearly at this stage you want Ambulance. Be prepared to tell them where you are, which crossroad is the closest and what has happened. Do not hang up until they tell you to do so.

Make sure that you and other passengers are safe and not in a position where you and they may be hurt by other vehicles. If possible, move your car to a position where it is not obstructing traffic and does not pose a risk to other drivers. Do not endanger yourself by doing this.

Get down the details

Speak to the other driver, if there is one, and make a record of:
- Their name and contact number
- The make, model, colour and registration of their car
- The name of their insurance company.

Photographing their licence and the damaged car(s) and licence plates is an easy way of doing this.

If there are witnesses, get their contact details as well. This will be useful if there is a dispute about culpability.

Move your car

If your car if driveable, ring and see if you can find a friend to come without their own car to drive you and your car home, so that you don't have to drive yourself. The high levels of adrenaline in your body resulting from an accident can impair your decision-making skills and make it dangerous for you to drive home.

If your car is not driveable, you will need to ring your insurance company. If there is a dispute about who is at fault, ring the police and request their attendance – they will produce an incident report that can subsequently be called upon by the insurance companies at a later date.

Submit your claim...

Some insurance companies have an App where you can submit photographs directly from your smart phone via the app to start the claims process. You can download it on the spot and start the claims process on the side of the road.

If the damage is large and you haven't yet contacted your insurance company, when you get home settle down, then ring them or contact them through their website. You don't need to know your policy number – they can search on your name or your car's rego. You should do this whether it is you or the other person who is at fault. They will handle it from there on in.

...or organise your own repairs

But if your car is only slightly damaged and it's not worth going through the insurance company, make sure you get several quotes for repairs from panel beaters or mechanics. There can be a wide range of prices charged for the same repairs.

How To Maintain Your Car

Cleaning your car

You should clean your car at least once a month. Either go to one of those car wash places and have fun with a couple of dollars and a high pressure hose, or do it at home using the following procedure.

Inside

Clean the inside of the car first. Take out the rubber mats and wash them in warm, soapy water and leave them against the fence to dry. Throw away any rubbish you find inside the car. Vacuum the carpet and the seats, using a long thin vacuum attachment so that you can get into all the nooks and crannies and around the pedals. If you can, use your normal vacuum cleaner rather than a hand-held one – the latter doesn't have enough power to do a really good job. Put on the soft brush attachment and vacuum the dashboard.

You can use plastic cleaner to clean the dashboard and leather cleaner for leather seats, but warm soapy water on a very well wrung-out cloth can be a good alternative. Be careful as too much water can be a disaster for electrical components if it seeps through. It's not that great for fabric seats either, so be careful and wring out your cloth well.

Wipe the rear-vision mirror and clean the inside of all the windows. You're done. Now on to the outside.

Outside

If you can, park the car on some lawn that needs a good drink. Spray the outside well with a hose, then use a soft brush or a sponge and warm soapy water in a bucket to clean the whole of the car, starting at the top and working down. If you're using a sponge, make sure you wring it out before putting it back in the bucket to avoid dirtying the water.

Hose the whole car down again to remove loosened dirt and suds, then squeegee the windows clean. Finally, dry the whole car, either with a chamois or a couple of old towels. You can put some polish on after this, which basically involves putting it on and rubbing it off using quite a lot of elbow grease – read the instructions on the bottle. You can also use some tyre spray to make the tyres black – looks very gangsta!

Tyre Care

In order to maximise the life of your tyres you should:"

- It is a legal requirement[56] that tyres have more than 1.5 mm of tread. When tread wears, the tyre's ability to disperse water decreases and your stopping distance increases
- Make sure you have the right inflation pressure for your tyre. Look for the manufacturer's recommended pressure on the sticker on the driver's side door pillar or fuel flap
- Check your tyre pressure when your tyres are cold. Increase pressure for heavy loads or sustained high speeds
- Like everything, tyres age – check the tyre's age by looking at the Tyre Identification Number (TIN). The last four digits indicate the week and year the tyre was made e.g. a tyre with TIN XXX4804 was made in the 48th week of 2004
- Rotate your tyres regularly and at least every 5000 to 8000kms. Rotating tyres mean that they wear evenly
- Get a professional wheel alignment every 6 months. A worn tyre increases the time it takes to brake in the wet.

Your car will handle better and use less petrol when the tyres have the correct inflation pressure. Your car handbook will tell you what this pressure should be (or a quick search of the Internet will do the same). Every service station will have an air hose to refill your tyres. Unscrew the little cap on your tyre, push on the far end of the metal handpieces until it seals, then read the pressure off the dial. If the pressure is too low, depress the lever without disconnecting the hand piece from the tyre. (On some hoses you do not need to depress a lever – air will be added automatically).

Don't forget to screw on the little plastic cap again!

How to open the bonnet

Make sure the car is off and it is parked on a flat surface with the handbrake on. If you've never done this before, it is a 2-step process. You need to undo the latch while you are still seated inside the car – it is usually around knee height on the door side, but if you can't find it, check your owner's manual. You will need to pull it firmly and will hear a click outside. Then go to the front of the car, where you will notice that the bonnet is now slightly ajar. Standing directly in front of the car (in the middle), slide your hand in between the bonnet and the car, and depress the little lever you will feel, and while still depressing it, lift the bonnet. Support it open with the long stick which is lying horizontally at the front of the engine – it will fit into an opening on the underneath of the bonnet and hold it up.

How to check the water

The radiator is one of the main parts of the cooling system of your car and contains liquid that circulates through the system i.e. 'coolant'. If you see the high temperature warning display on your dashboard, stop driving and take care of it immediately.

Before checking anything under the bonnet of the car it is good practice to familiarise yourself with the engine bay layout by reading the owner's manual that comes with your car.

If your car is fitted with an expansion tank (a plastic coolant reservoir) check that the coolant level is at – or slightly above – the 'minimum' mark when the engine is cold, or somewhere between the half and 'maximum' marks with the engine at normal (hot) operating temperature..

If your car is not fitted with an expansion tank (typically older vehicles), check the coolant (or water) is within about 25mm of the top of the filler neck when the engine is cold. Never attempt this with a hot car as the radiator contents are under pressure and you could end up with boiling water or hot coolant spurting in your face. To check the level, unscrew the radiator lid, which is found near the front of the engine. If it is an original lid, it will often be yellow and marked with words such as 'engine coolant', 'under pressure' or 'caution'. Sometimes these lids are lost and are then replaced with plastic ones that may or may not have any markings on them. The shape of the lid is usually round with a projection on either side.

Have a look inside – you should be able to see the fluid right near the top. If more coolant is required, the system should be topped up with a mixture of clean water and the recommended coolant/inhibitor. Make sure you screw the lid back on again.

Persistent coolant loss indicates a problem, which your mechanic should check immediately.

How to check the oil

Cars need oil to reduce the friction between the moving parts, and to help dissipate the heat caused by normal workings of the engine. If you don't keep the oil level up, things can go badly wrong.

To check the oil, open the bonnet (see page 176). Locate the oil dipstick which is a metal stick inserted deep into the engine – all you will see is a little finger sized metal or plastic loop that is sticking out. Pull the stick out, wipe it off with a cloth, reinsert it and pull it out again. Have a look at the level the oil has reached on the stick. The bottom end of the stick will have markings on it to indicate what level the engine oil is at – often with an 'L' (for low) on one end of the markings and an 'H' (for high) on the other. The level should be up towards the 'H'.

If it is down towards the 'L', start by adding a litre of oil. Buy the oil that is recommended in your owner's manual (they come in different grades). To add oil, unscrew the oil cap located on top of the engine and typically marked with 'OIL' or a picture of an oil can and pour in the oil, either with a funnel or straight out of the oil can. Now check the oil again to see that the level has risen and is now okay. If not, add more oil. Voila! Done!

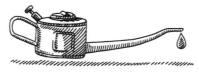

How to change a tyre

If you are a member of a motoring association or have paid your insurance company for roadside assistance, they will do this for you. If not and you think it's worth it, join now over the phone. Call them and wait.

If you are in a rush, are in a rural area so that help is not guaranteed to come, or just want to do it yourself, do the following:

1. Make sure the car is parked safely away from the line of traffic, on a flat piece of ground. Do not change a tyre on a hill!

2. Put the hand brake on and turn on the hazard lights

3. Get the spare tyre out of the boot

4. Find the tools in the boot of the car and use the flat end of the wrench to lever off the hubcap if there is one, then use the socket end of the wrench to just loosen each of the tyre bolts. Do not take them off at this stage

5. Locate the jack in the boot of the car, align it under the chassis of the car at the point indicated in the car's manual, and jack it up till the tyre clears the ground

6. Now completely loosen all the bolts, each bolt a bit at a time (i.e. not one bolt completely, then the others). Put the bolts in the upturned hubcap or in a pile together on the ground

7. Gently pull the tyre straight towards you and lay it on the ground

8. Pick up the spare tyre and push it on as far as it can go

9. Gently put on each of the bolts by hand (each one a little at a time, doing ones opposite each other in turn), and then tighten with the socket end of the wrench

10. Lower the jack carefully and tighten all the bolts completely with the wrench, again opposites in turn

11. Replace the hubcap and put the flat tyre in the boot. Put the tools back in the car, and check that you haven't left anything on the ground.

12. In the next day or so, have the tyre repaired. Don't drive around for weeks with a flat tyre as it's a sure invitation to get another one. And if it's a temporary space saver tyre, check the manual for restrictions – usually a limited number of kilometres, a lower maximum speed and no towing.

How to deal with a scratch

So, someone's keyed your car while you were in the supermarket. What a pain. Grab some nail polish in the same colour as your car (or Liquid Paper if it's white), and carefully paint in the scratch. From a distance and with a bit of a squint it might look as good as new.

Another method is slightly more involved and will end up with a better result, but will only work if you can't see any primer or even worse bare metal in the scratch. If so, forget it and revert to the first option above, or get the panel professionally resprayed.

Wash the scratch with soapy water and then sand it with very fine (minimum 2000 grit) wet and dry sandpaper and lots of water till the scratch and the surrounding metal are at the at same level. Then use a liquid buffing compound on a cloth to get rid of any scratches left by the sandpaper, and then hand buff with a soft cloth. Finally use car wax to seal it.

Okay, let's be realistic here, neither method will be perfect but it should look better than it did…

Servicing

Servicing is a drag. Servicing is expensive. Servicing means that your car is safe, that it lasts longer and that it uses less fuel, and a complete service book will mean your car will be more appealing to a potential buyer when you decide to upgrade. No more needs to be said, but stick to your servicing schedule!

Driving economy

This is not the most appealing of topics and if you are reading this, congratulations for getting this far! You can absolutely guarantee that petrol prices are not going to go down in the near future, so to minimise your petrol use:

- Accelerate and brake smoothly
- Drop a few km/h off the speed you are travelling
- Don't carry excess baggage in your boot (such as skis or golf clubs)
- Maintain your tyres at the manufacturer-recommended tyre pressure
- Make any friends who regularly drive in your car lose weight. (Not really – I just added this in to see if you were still reading)
- Take off roof racks or luggage pods when not in use
- Keep your car well serviced
- Walk or ride and use your car less. Good for the environment, good for your health.

And Finally, Driving And The Law

Driving fines are administered by State Governments and are not designed to increase revenue for the government but to decrease risky driving (yes, really!). If you are caught breaking the law while driving (for instance, by touching your mobile phone) you will incur demerit points and a fine. If you earn too many demerit points you will lose your licence. For instance, in some states if you are a probationary driver, you will lose your licence for going 35km/h or more above the speed limit.

Speeding is a common reason to be pulled over by the police and this is because an increase in speed is correlated with an increase in accidents. If you drive at 5km/h above the speed limit of 60km/h you double your chance of being involved in an accident resulting in a casualty[57].

Local councils administer parking infringements and you do not incur demerit points for these – just a pesky fine. These can totally destroy your budget, so always check the parking sign carefully when you stop your car and in particular, avoid clearways at all costs. If you park in a clearway at the designated time you will come back to find that your car has been towed away and it will cost you an arm and a leg (not to mention a taxi fare to the depot where your car is being held) to get it back.

If you are on a restricted probationary licence, you will need to be familiar with the restrictions placed on drivers. Again, these vary from state to state[58], but will generally include:

- A zero blood-alcohol content
- No use of a mobile phone, including hands free devices
- A limit on the number of peer passengers you can carry
- A restriction on the type of car you may drive. At the time of writing, this was moving from restrictions on the number of cylinders and turbo chargers, to restricting power-to-weight ratios
- A lower maximum speed limit (e.g. 90km/h in NSW).

Five Top Tips

1. Check out the ANCAP star rating for the safety of any car you are thinking of buying

2. Do a search on the VIN (Vehicle Identification Number) of any car you are interested in to see if it's been stolen, written off or has money owing against it

3. If you are involved in an accident, use your smart phone to photograph the licence of the other person, their number plate and any damage to the cars

4. Air pressure of tyres is important. You should check it when it's cold and increase it for heavy loads or high speeds

5. Use nail polish to disguise a scratch and Liquid Paper if your car is white. It won't be perfect but looks better than nothing and protects the car from rusting until you choose to get it fixed.

CHAPTER 11

THERE'S SOMETHING FURRY LIVING WITH US

You've grown up with a dog and a couple of cats at home and your new place seems empty without a pet. But before you jump in and buy Felix or Fido, there are a few things to consider.

Haven't Got Time To Read The Whole Chapter? Read This.

1. Pets require a huge commitment of time – think 12 years for the average pet and 20 years for some. What will you be doing in two decades' time?

2. Be aware that some breeds are 'cheap to run' while others have inherent problems. Can you cope with a depressed American Shorthair cat or a Poodle with Glaucoma?

3. Houses can be dangerous places for pets – Aspirin, chocolate, onions, Panadol, Aloe and Cyclamens are all toxic to both dogs and cats

4. Got $25,000 in your pocket? On average, that's how much it will cost to own a dog over its lifetime according to the Australian Veterinary Association

5. If you go away, cats can stay happily at home alone for up to a week if they are fed and watered; dogs are not happy at all if left alone for any length of time.

Thinking Of Getting A Pet?

If you're thinking about buying a little fluffy companion, make sure you sit down and have a big think. Think about the commitment of time that a pet requires (feeding, exercising and health care) as well as the significant commitment in money.

You'll also need to consider whether a pet will fit into your lifestyle (do you travel a lot? Do you stay out late at night?) and your living space (will your landlord allow pets?). Do your research before you jump in, and remember that pets can live for a long time. The RSPCA says that the average pet lives for 12 years[59] but some smaller pets can live for up to 20 years.

CASE STUDY: A DOG IS FOR LIFE

Nicky bought her Jack Russell puppy, Clover, when she was 22 years old, single and living in an apartment. When she got married at 31, Clover was still a sprightly 9 year old and by the time Clover was at the end of her life Nicky was 42 and had three children at school.

What will you be doing in 20 years? Will your pet still suit you and your lifestyle then?

Lesson: Think of the future when buying a pet

Breed

Get on line and have a look at the pets out there – there are all sorts of breeds with all sorts of different characteristics and one may be perfect for you. You should bear in mind that many breeds have particular health problems e.g. Bulldogs can have respiratory problems, German Shepherds can have hip problems, Labradors get fat, Golden Retrievers get skin allergies, and Poodles get Glaucoma. With cats, Birmans become overweight, Persians have heart problems, Abysinnians have stress-related hair loss and American Shorthairs get depressed! Choose carefully and don't be swayed by their cute little faces.

Where do you get your pet?

Either buy your pet from a breeder, or from a shelter. With a breeder you are sure of what you are getting and the breeder is as concerned as you are that the relationship works. In fact, they may want to check you out as much as you want to check them out! Pets bought from breeders can cost anywhere from a couple of hundred dollars, to several thousands.

If you buy from a shelter you will feel good that you are saving a dog or cat's life, but remember that there may have been issues that caused the pet to be abandoned in the first place. If you decide this is a good option for you, look for a not-for-profit outfit such as the RSPCA or the Animal Welfare League of Australia's state operations – they have re-homing services where the cost of buying a de-sexed and micro-chipped animal ranges from around $200 to $350, depending on whether you are after a cat or a dog, and the age of the animal.

Don't ever buy from...

Whatever you do, there are two places where you should not buy a pet. The first is from a pet shop, as these pets were probably bred on a puppy farm. Their mother has most likely spent her whole life either gestating or lactating in terrible conditions. Apart from the moral issues of supporting this type of puppy production, you have no guarantee about the nature or health of the ensuing puppy, many of whom have serious illnesses.

The second place not to buy a puppy is from a puppy farm over the Internet. Always buy from a breeder. The trouble is that it can be hard to tell if a website belongs to a breeder or a puppy farm.

Checklist: Breeders vs. puppy farms

Does this website belong to a breeder? Check:
- That they are selling only one or two types of dogs. (Puppy farms will be selling a number of different breeds.)
- That they are involved in other dog-related activities such as education or showing. (Puppy farms are only concerned with selling puppies.)
- That they are concerned about who you are and whether you are suited to having one of their dogs. (Puppy farms only want to make money.)
- By visiting the premises if it is feasible. (Puppy farms will not let you have a look around.)

Costs

Guess how much the average pet will cost you over its lifetime? $5,000? $10,000? Think again.

Approximate costs for pets at the time of publication, include:
- Purchasing the animal (ranging from around $200 to over $3000)
- De-sexing (up to $275 for dogs and $220 for cats)
- Immunisations (an annual fee of around $160 for cats and $240 for dogs)
- Annual registration (if de-sexed, $50 for dogs and $32 for cats; if not, $153 for dogs and $100 for cats)
- Clipping (from $40, several times a year)
- And if you or your house isn't up to it, bathing ($25)

So what does this add up to?

Approx. Lifetime* Cost of Owning a Pet	Annual Cost	Lifetime Cost
Purchase		$500
De-sexing		$275
Puppy School		$250
Micro-chipping		$80
Immunisation	$240	$2,880
Worms & Fleas	$100	$1,200
Registration	$50	$600
Clipping	$120	$1,440
Bathing	$75	$900
Vet Fees		$2,500
Kennel costs	$175	$2,100
Food	$450	$5,400
Toys/Leads	$50	$1,200
Beds		$200
	TOTAL	$19,525

*Assuming the pet lives for the average 12 years

If you think this is unreasonable, it's not! The Family Pooch Index of the Australian Veterinary Association[60] actually suggests that the cost of owning a dog for its lifespan will be more than $25,000, with Gen Y as a group spending more than any other group on their pets.

What else do cats and dogs need?

Apart from the collar, tag, leash and toys you'll need to think about a bed of some sort and a car restraint or carry box.

Cats will need litter trays. The general rule is that you need one litter tray per cat plus one extra, which means that two cats require three litter trays. This is because cats can be quite fussy and think that a used litter tray is like a dirty public toilet.

You will also need to think about storage space for food. Animal food is significantly cheaper to buy in bulk but do you have the room to store a 15kg bag of dog food?

Food

You can choose either wet or dry food but make sure it is balanced. It will say so on the label, or you can ask your vet.

When considering which food to use, remember that dry food has many (mainly poo-related) advantages. Dry food usually results in less faeces and the faeces itself is less smelly. That's got to be a good thing.

The poo is also firmer so it is easier to remove from the litter tray or pick up in a plastic poo bag. And finally, because the food is more nutritionally dense, the volumes of food required are smaller and so it is easier to carry the food home and to store once you get there.

Premium or economy food?

Just as in a human's diet, with pets there is healthy everyday food and not-so-healthy occasional food. While you can treat your pet with cheap supermarket pet snacks, with everyday food you should aim to go for a premium brand. Try to go for one that is locally made – it's cheaper and think of all those food miles you are saving!

Premium brands are more expensive than supermarket brands. While it may not seem a wise economic decision, it probably is. You will buy premium food less often because you feed your pet less of it each day due to its high nutritional density. You will also be sure that you are doing the right thing nutritionally by your pet and as a result, they may suffer less from dietary upsets.

Daily feeding routine

Up to the age of six months, you should feed cats and dogs three times per day. This does not necessarily mean at breakfast, lunch and dinner time, but ideally would be at intervals of around eight hours' apart (say 8am, 5:30pm and 11pm). Some cats may be good at grazing, in which case you can leave food in their bowl for them to eat throughout the day. Most dogs are not good grazers and however much you put into their bowl, it will be gone in two minutes.

After six months, you can revert to twice a day feeding. Always make sure you have fresh clean water available at all times.

One thing – do not feed cats on dog food. Yes, it's tempting because it is cheaper but it is too low in protein and fat, and does not contain Taurine, an amino acid that cats are unable to manufacture themselves. If fed exclusively on dog food, cats can end up with heart problems.

Poo

How do you feel about poo? You'll need to get used to it if you have a pet. The fine for not picking up after your dog can be around $250, depending on your local council.

So how do you do it? For dogs, using a poo bag, turn the bag inside out, put your hand in it, then pick up the poo and turn the bag back out the right way out. Voila! Poo on the inside and hand (hopefully clean) on the outside. Tie it up and throw it into a council rubbish bin.

Most parks have free bags or you can buy a roll of them from the pet shop. Be warned, biodegradable ones make you feel good but sometimes split with less than appealing results.

With cats, if you use a clumping litter it is easy to extract the poo as it forms discreet lumps. Use the same technique with the poo bag as above.

Keeping Your Pet Healthy

The following is advice from a vet but please note that the circumstances of your own pet may differ so consult your local practice for specific information.

Immunisations for cats

Immunisations for cats are required at around six-eight weeks, at 12 weeks, at 16 weeks and then annually. In some circumstances, immunisations are only required every three years after the initial kitten vaccinations.

Cats require either F3 (for Feline Enteritis plus two respiratory diseases, formally referred to as Cat 'Flu) or F4 (which is F3 plus treatment for Chlamydophila, an eye problem which was previously known as Chlamydia).

Outdoor cats also need treatment for FIV (similar to HIV), a virus that can lead to feline AIDS.

Immunisations for dogs

Immunisations for dogs are also required at around six-eight weeks, at 12 weeks, at 16 weeks and then annually.

Dogs require either C3 (for Distemper, Hepatitis and Parvo Virus) or C5 (which is C3 plus immunisation against two canine coughs). C5 is recommended if the dog lives in a built up area or will be mixing with lots of other dogs.

Worms

All pets also need a regular annual intestinal worming treatment (such as Milbemax for cats or Drontal for dogs). And all dogs also need heartworm treatment.

Fleas

When it comes to fleas, the case is not so clear-cut. Some people are horrified by fleas and will always treat their pets, even if the pets do not go outside. Some people will only treat for fleas over summer when fleas are more prevalent. And some people will only treat when there is an indication that their pet has fleas, such as when they scratch and lick themselves more than normal, or when you can see the little blighters by separating the fur and having a good look.

To treat fleas, there are both tablets and spot-on treatments. These can treat just for fleas alone, or treat for fleas plus intestinal worms and/or heartworms. One reason to keep fleas under control (apart from keeping them out of your carpets!) is that an animal's skin can become sensitised if they are repeatedly bitten and they may develop an allergy to the saliva in the flea's bite. If this occurs, the ensuing skin condition will have to be treated over the long term, maybe for the rest of the pet's life.

Common Cat Complaints

The things that might concern your cat, or which will make you take Moggy to see the vet can include:

Hairballs

Cats groom themselves and as a result can ingest their own fur. Occasionally this may be vomited up as tube of matted, slimy hair. Think Puss in Boots in *Shrek 2* and you'll get an idea why this is best avoided for both you and your cat. Grooming your cat often and feeding it a special hairball food can help.

Fight wounds

Cats can suffer from fight wounds when they are out and about. Apart from the fact that it may be the law to keep your cat inside after dusk, this is a good reason to stop them from roaming the streets at night. Depending on the wounds, the cat might require antibiotics or surgery.

Respiratory tract infections

Like us, cats can get colds with symptoms such as a cough, a runny nose and eyes, and mouth ulcers. Generally these infections are viral and your main job is to keep the cat well-hydrated and comfortable.

Bad teeth

Cats' teeth are hard to clean with a toothbrush (no, I'm not joking, you can get cat toothbrushes) so to avoid bad teeth you can try a couple of things. Give them raw chicken bones to crunch on. Or try specific foods for tooth care that have larger kibble and are less brittle. This allows the tooth to be inserted further into each piece and therefore cleans it as the cat eats.

Being hit by a car

I'm not sure I need to say anything here. Keep your cat in at night; it's the law and sensible, too.

Arthritis

Like humans, cats suffer from age-related, degenerative (wearing down) arthritis that causes them pain, stiffness and disfiguration. It can make them grumpy, too. Treat this by weight-loss, physiotherapy and drugs such as corticosteroids and painkillers.

Poisoning

Many household items and plants are toxic to cats – please see the list on page 190-191.

Common Dog Complaints

Cuts from running into things

Dogs get lacerations from running into things – like the sharp edges of a piece of furniture or a park bench. These can need stitches and/or antibiotics.

Being hit by a car

All dogs should be kept on a leash except in leash-free areas. Even if you are just crossing the road to see your neighbour, always put your dog on a leash. Your dog may be extremely well trained, but can still be distracted by a cat or a particularly interesting dog on the other side of the road.

Gastroenteritis

Dogs are scavengers and often get gastroenteritis ('gastro') from scavenging when out and about (Cat poo! Dead animals! Left over sandwiches!) or from eating too much of a good thing. Treatment involves keeping the pet well hydrated, and reintroducing bland food such as boiled rice and steamed chicken in small doses. In worse cases, your vet may give an injection to stop vomiting and insert a drip to keep your pet hydrated.

Canine cough

While dogs get less respiratory infections than cats, they can get the highly infectious Canine Cough (previously known as Kennel Cough). The dog will have a persistent and strong cough but will generally not be off his food. This will normally resolve by itself although your vet may give your pet antibiotics.

Arthritis

Dogs can also suffer from age-related arthritis due to the wearing down of their joints. This can be very painful, making them stiff and grumpy. Treatment can involve painkillers, corticosteroids, physiotherapy and weight loss.

Keeping Your Pet Safe

There are a number of common household items and plants that are toxic to cats and dogs so be careful around the house.

Household items that are toxic to your animals

Item		Dogs	Cats
Aspirin	Even just one tablet	Toxic	Toxic
Chocolate	Contains Theobromine which can cause seizures and may result in death. Dark chocolate is worse than white. Cats don't like chocolate so less of a risk for them	Toxic	Toxic
Grapes & raisins	May lead to kidney failure	Toxic	
Onions (and related plants such as chives & garlic)	Can damage red blood cells leading to anaemia and also gastrointestinal problems	Toxic	Toxic
Macadamia nuts		Toxic	

Panadol (Paracetamol)	Can cause anaemia, ulcers and lead to kidney and liver failure	Toxic	Toxic
Napthalene mothballs	May kill pets (and they're not too great for us either)	Toxic	Toxic
Household chemicals (cleaners, garden chemicals and pest poisons)		Toxic	Toxic

Plants that are toxic to animals

Lilies are very toxic to cats (even the pollen) and slightly less toxic to dogs. They may cause heart problems possibly resulting in death. Cyclamens are also toxic to both cats and dogs and can cause vomiting and diarrhoea.

Jade Plants can cause vomiting, depression, a slowing heart rate and unconsciousness and Corn Plants, Philodendrons, Aloe and Elephant's Ear are all toxic to both dogs and cats.

Should I call the vet?

You wake up and your cat is behaving weirdly. She's listless and off her food. Should you go to the vet?

My advice is to develop a relationship with your local vet before your pet becomes very ill. Go and visit the clinic and get to know the staff. Then when you need advice, you can give the clinic a call. You probably won't get to speak to the vet straight away, but the nurses are very good at phone triage and can tell you if what you have is an emergency or if it's more a 'wait and see' type problem.

Being responsible

- Keep your dog on a lead unless it is in an off-leash area
- Micro-chip and register both cats and dogs
- Keep cats inside overnight to protect themselves from fighting and from cars, and also to keep them from hunting native animals
- Enrol your puppy in classes for socialisation.

Emergency 24-hour centres

There are lots of emergency 24-hour centres and you should try to find one that is close to your house. Check with your usual clinic to see if they have a relationship with one, or one that they particularly recommend. Be warned that some emergency clinics might offer a more comprehensive service than the situation warrants or than you are used to. You can end up spending a fortune.

Pet insurance

Your vet would most likely recommend pet insurance – it can be only a couple of dollars a week for a whole lot of peace of mind. Make sure you look at the excess which will be charged (this is the amount you yourself must pay when you make a claim, before payment from the insurance company kicks in). Also check for breeds which may be excluded from a policy, and exclusions which are related to the age of your pet.

Give your own health fund or household insurer a ring to see if they have pet insurance. This can make the whole business a lot cheaper. It is worth noting here that the RSPCA also offers pet insurance.

CASE STUDY: PET INSURANCE IN ACTION

Amber, the 10–year-old Labrador was a bit of a wuss, and in particular was afraid of thunderstorms. One day a huge storm ravaged Adelaide and she escaped from her back yard, running directly across the road outside and was hit by a car. She needed x-rays of her hip (requiring a general anaesthetic and a day in hospital) for $570. Her subsequent hip surgery, including medication, cost $5,500 which came to a total of $6,070. Her owners were very happy they had taken out pet insurance to cover this initial cost, and any potential ongoing costs.

Lesson: A couple of dollars a week in pet insurance can pay dividends

---

De-sexing Your Pet

And now a word on the de-sexing of pets. Whether you call it castration, spaying, fixing or giving the snip, your vet would recommend it for animals that are not going to be used for showing or breeding. In fact, in some areas it is a Council regulation that all cats be de-sexed[61].

There are a number of good reasons why you should consider de-sexing your animals.

1. Council registration is cheaper for a de-sexed pet, at around one third of the cost of an intact pet

2. De-sexing tends to make both males and females less dominant, aggressive and prone to wandering

3. Your pets may become more affectionate and your pets can't get cancer or infections of the reproductive organs

4. You avoid the mess of females coming on heat and potentially the arrival of kittens and puppies

5. And here's a big one: it will stop the marking of territories. That's when your pet wees around the place to show that it's the boss. Yuk.

What To Do If You Go Away

Cats

Cats can be happily left in the house while you go away for up to a week, as long as someone can come in twice a day. The morning visit is to feed and water them, to clean up the kitty litter and to let them out for the day. The night-time visit is to feed and water them again, to clean up the kitty litter and to lock them in for the night.

If you are away for more than a week, cats will become stressed, so you must either put them into a cattery (at the time of writing, around $16 a day), or organise for someone to move in. Cats are not particularly happy to move into someone else's house for a short period of time or to go on holiday with you, as they are generally very attached to their houses and moving can be very disturbing for them.

Dogs

Dogs are not happily left alone for any period of time at all. You will need to take them with you, re-house them with someone familiar (make sure they can't escape), have someone move in to look after them, or put them into a kennel. This can cost around $25 a day.

How to find a good kennel

Your vet clinic may offer a cat-minding service and they may also be able to recommend a good cattery or kennel. Pet-owning friends can offer good advice, but be warned that many catteries and kennels are situated outside major metropolitan areas and may involve a long drive or a costly pick-up and delivery service. If possible you should organise a visit to meet the staff and look at the facilities, and make sure that you test the kennel or cattery for a weekend stay before you plan a longer one.

So that's it! I hope that you and your pet have a long and happy life together.

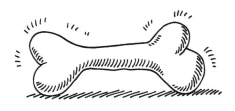

Five Top Tips

1. Buy your pets from a pet breeder or shelter. Don't ever look for pets in a pet shop or on-line – they're likely to be from a puppy farm

2. Dry food will result in poo that is smaller, dryer and less smelly. Go dry!

3. Don't feed cats on dog food as it can result in them having heart problems

4. As well as the annual immunisations of F3 or F5 (for cats) and C3 or C5 (for dogs), all pets need a regular intestinal worm treatment

5. Get your pet de-sexed. Council registration is cheaper for de-sexed animals, and your pet will most likely be less dominant and more affectionate.

With many thanks to Dr Donald Ward for his help in writing this chapter.

THINGS WITH LEAVES AND STEMS

Your apartment's a mess. Your love life's a disaster. Your job's going nowhere. And you're not even sure the cat likes you anymore. Never fear! A bunch of flowers on the kitchen bench can make everything seem all right.

Haven't Got Time To Read The Whole Chapter? Read This.

1. The best place to buy fresh flowers is at a wholesale market where turnover is high; the worst is from a street-side vendor where the flowers can be affected by wind, light and pollution

2. Modern fake flowers are surprisingly lovely and you can mix them with a smaller bunch of fresh flowers for an impressive display at little ongoing cost

3. Tropical plants make a good choice to have inside as they enjoy a warmer temperature

4. Generally smaller household plants will need to be re-potted every year, with larger ones needing to be done every two years

5. The easiest herbs to grow are the perennial ones – once planted (and looked after!) they will keep on growing for years. Parsley, Thyme, Rosemary and Mint are all good choices.

Buying Flowers

Your choice of flower will determine how long you have them in your house – some will last for weeks and others will be here and gone in a couple of days. Choose carefully, particularly if you have a limited budget.

Longest lasting flowers

The longest lasting flowers (although they can be tricky to find) are those that grow in arid areas, such as everlasting daisies (e.g. paper daisy) and Statice. They can be very colourful, will last for several weeks in your vase and if you hang them upside down to dry first, they can last for years. Can't beat that.

Orchids, Lilies Chrysanthemums and Carnations are also a good choice. Lilies can last for up to two weeks if you get them when they are tightly budded. Similarly Alstroemeria (Peruvian Lilies) last extremely well, are very cheap and come in a huge range of colours. Don't buy them if you have cats, as all lilies are extremely toxic to your feline friends.

Orchids, Lilies, Chrysanthemums and Carnations are all generally easily available, are budget friendly and even better, if they are white you can stick them in water coloured with food dye and they will change colour. Cool – a living science experiment!

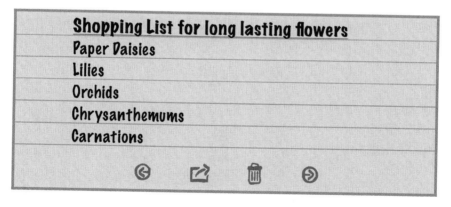

Shopping List for long lasting flowers
Paper Daisies
Lilies
Orchids
Chrysanthemums
Carnations

Enjoy, but don't get too attached

Roses are probably the best known of all flowers and you can buy them everywhere – from the petrol station to the high-end florist. They come in a huge range of colours and varieties and can be reasonably priced. Gerberas, too, are widely available and are also quite inexpensive. These two types of flowers are good solid investments as long as they are fresh, and should see out a week on your kitchen bench.

Forget it

Tulips and Irises are for the rich or insane. Don't be tempted by them. Those beautiful Tulips are exquisite but in a day or so you will see them weeping their petals onto the table. The same with Irises – they will break your heart.

Air cleaning plants & flowers

If you are looking to keep the air inside your place clean, some plants act as air purifiers, and these include Chrysanthemums, Peace Lilies, English Ivy, Bamboo Palm and Gerberas.

Where to buy them

The best place to buy flowers is at a wholesale market – some vendors are happy to sell to individuals as long as you don't on-sell the flowers yourself. The next best place is a florist, and you should be very happy if they are presented in glass containers (black plastic buckets hide a multitude of sins). The worst place to buy them is from a street vendor with buckets on the side of the road, or any location that is exposed to light, wind or pollution.

Surprisingly flowers at the supermarket can be a good buy. They are invariably cheap and if you find out what day they come in, can be very fresh. Don't buy ones that have been marked down – they're cheap because they're one step off dead.

What to look for when buying flowers

Although this can be hard to see if the flowers are in black plastic buckets, look for clean water and tightly budded flowers. Having a surreptitious sniff of the water can make you seem very weird but will tell you as much as looking at them. Leaves should be firm with no browning on the edges.

Ideally you want to buy flowers from a shop that has a high turnover so go for a popular shop with lots of pedestrian traffic. If you can, find out when your local flower seller gets their fresh flowers in. It will not be every day and if you coincide your buying with the day the florist goes to the market, you should have longer lasting flowers in your house.

Fake flowers

Are you thinking retirement village entrance hall, or doctor's surgery? Don't! There are some really beautiful ones on the market such as Lilies, Magnolias and Peonies and you'll need to touch them to tell them apart from their genuine floral sisters. But be warned – they are horribly expensive, even up to several hundred dollars for a bunch. Save up for them, then mix them with a smaller bunch of fresh flowers for an impressive display at a reasonable cost.

Keeping Flowers

Transporting flowers

If you are transporting flowers any distance, make sure they have a wet paper towel wrapped around the end of the stems, covered by a plastic bag securely tired on to avoid drips. Keep them out of the heat and sun, ideally in a slightly cool temperature. Make sure that they are adequately supported, not rolling around in the back of your car! And put them in water as soon as you can.

Help! My flowers haven't opened!

So, you've bought a great bunch of flowers to have on display at your dinner party tonight. Trouble is the flowers are all shut and the arrangement looks like a bunch of sticks in a vase.

To overcome this you can try a few things: put warm (not hot) water in the vase, gently pull the buds apart at the tip (only do this if the bud has started to open, otherwise you'll end up pulling them to pieces) or blow on them. Yep, blow on them! These methods won't always work but you've got the best chance with Roses and Lilies.

How to make them last

To make flowers last, try the following:

- If you are lucky enough to be picking flowers from your own garden, pick them in the early morning or late afternoon. They'll be much fresher and will last longer. Always cut the stems on a slant and with secateurs as this gives a clean cut and the greatest surface area from which the flower can absorb water
- If you are buying flowers, when you get them home cut off their stems at an angle with secateurs, removing around 2cm from the bottom. Try not to use a knife – you'll wreck both the flowers AND the knife!
- If the flower has a woody stem, remove the outer wood for 7cm from the end of the stalk to allow water to be absorbed
- Remove any leaves that will end up below the water line. They'll quickly turn manky and the water will smell disgusting
- Immediately put them in clean water to which has been added sugar or lemonade (to provide nourishment) and either a splash of white vinegar, bleach or vodka (which all reduce bacterial growth). Don't overdose as you'll end up with dead flowers (or at least drunk ones)
- Alternatively, you can add an aspirin to the water (½ an aspirin if it's a small vase)
- Ideally, you should change the flower water each day, cutting the stems again, and washing out the vase with hot soapy water to remove all bacteria. Realistically if you can do this every couple of days and just top up the water in between, you'll be half way there
- Make sure that the water covers the shortest stem in the bunch – usually ¾ of the way up the vase is a good choice.

How else do I keep them fresh?

Keep them out of draughts and away from heat sources such as direct sunlight or heaters. At night put them into the coolest room of the house (often the bathroom) or outside, but not in the fridge. Heat will cause the flowers to open too quickly and this is what we are trying to avoid.

Displaying Flowers

What vases do I need?

Personally I never seem to have exactly the right vase to display my flowers – they're always too short, too fat, too narrow, too tall. But remember you can use almost any container, and repetition can be the key to a beautiful arrangement. Try an odd number (yep, weird, but always has to be odd) of the same type of jam jar with a flower in each. Or perhaps an old jug, or pewter mug, or even a fish-bowl.

If you are sticking to real vases, go for clear glass ones. At a minimum you will need:

- A small narrow 10cm vase for a single flower
- A tall large vase for an arrangement of flowers such as lilies
- A couple of medium size squat vases for posies.

Checklist: How do I clean a vase?

Hot soapy water with a bottle brush is ideal but for stubborn stains take your pick of the following:

- Try a denture-cleaning tablet dissolved in water. You can buy these in a box quite cheaply at the supermarket and they work a treat. (And for you multi-taskers out there, they're also great for those brown stains in coffee cups. As well as for your false teeth.)
- Add a teaspoon of old-fashioned bicarbonate of soda to some warm water in a vase. Add vinegar till it fizzes then shake and rinse
- Sprinkle dishwashing powder into the vase, then add a little water. Shake it all about (doing the Hokey-Pokey if you want) and rinse
- Or if you are a tea drinker, fill the vase with tealeaves, add a little water and then cover the top with your hand. Shake vigorously and rinse.

How to make a posy

Start with your feature flower, or if you don't have one, your foliage. Holding the posy, spin it around, sliding in your other flowers and foliage, starting with the largest and moving to the smallest, and trying to keep it even from all angles of view. Generally, you should have an odd number of your feature flowers, say five or seven.

Tie the posy up with either string (which florists would advise) or rubber bands (which are easy and practical). When you are finished, the stems below your tying point should be in the shape of a clown's hat and the posy should be able to stand up on the bench by itself. If you are giving it away, tell the recipient not to take off the elastic band as it will collapse and lose its shape.

How to do a simple vase arrangement

Place your foliage in the vase, and then individually insert your focal flowers. These should be evenly spaced, say in the shape of a diamond (4 flowers) plus one flower in the middle. The total number of focal flowers should be odd.

Add in the other flowers you have chosen so that size and colour are balanced when looking at the arrangement from the front.

How to wrap flowers in paper

First fold your paper in half but a bit askew, so the edges don't match. Lay your posy down with the flowers almost reaching the unfolded edges, and the stems towards the fold. Roll the posy along the bench. Finally secure with tape down the edge, and a ribbon or raffia around the waist of the posy.

Indoor Plants

Instead of flowers, you can always go for an indoor plant. Flowering tropical plants make a good choice to have inside as they enjoy a warmer temperature. Phaelenopsis Orchids (those ones on the long tall stem) last forever if you treat them well and don't overwater them, and Cyclamens will grace your house for months on end, especially if you put them outside at night. (When they die, chuck them outside somewhere in their pots and forget them. Lo and behold! In a year's time they will surprise you with more flowers.)

Jade plants (Crassula Ovata), the succulents with the little squishy round green leaves, will survive almost anywhere. This is just as well because according to my Chinese friends they indicate your future wealth status – future wealth status! In particular they love full sunlight, and a good trim will make them bushier. Don't over water. You can re-plant the offcuts after leaving them for a week to harden, thereby making lots of little jade plants (and lots more money!).

White Anthurium love a temperature of around 20 degrees Celsius and are very happy in a bathroom, while needing little care and surviving massive neglect.

Checklist: Caring for indoor plants

- Read the little care tag that came with your plant – you can pretty safely assume that the person who grew it knows how to look after it
- Make sure they get enough light
- Water only as instructed, enough so that the leaves don't go brown and fall off, but not too much to drown it
- Talking about leaves going brown – cut them off! If you've been a bit distracted and there are lots of dead leaves, the plant might look a bit bald, but with a bit of luck it will recover
- If the leaves are yellow, it can be a sign of too much water
- Don't let the plant get wet feet. Make sure there are holes in the bottom of the pot. If it's a decorative one with no holes, grab a drill and a ceramic drill bit and put some in
- Look out for pests (on your plants I mean)
- Make sure you avoid any plants that are toxic to your animals
- And finally don't despair if you lose a plant or two – see it as an opportunity to try out something new.

Re-potting plants

If you are successful in not killing your pot-plants, at some stage they will need to be re-potted into a larger pot so that their roots do not become cramped. You can tell if a plant needs re-potting if it stops growing, or if you can see roots poking out through the drainage holes or up through the soil. Generally smaller household plants will need to be re-potted every year, with larger ones needing to be done every two years.

Here's how to do it, even if you can't reliably tell a stem from a root:

1. The day before, give the pot a good water. It's going to be an easier project if the soil is moist

2. Turn the pot upside down, and putting your fingers around the stem, give it a good shake. If the plant doesn't come out of the pot, give it a bang against the edge of a table

3. Once you have the plant out of the pot and upside down in your hands, tickle the roots, loosening them up. You will lose some soil but that's okay

4. If they are very tightly coiled, give the roots a trim

5. Put some potting mix in the bottom of your new pot, enough so that when you put in the plant it will be sitting at about the right level in the pot

6. Place the plant in, and then put potting mix all around, gently pushing it down. Continue until you have potting mix up to about 2.5cm (an inch) below the top of the pot

7. Give the pot a drink and have a cup of tea. Don't fertilise the pot for a month. Good job!

And a final word on herbs

However small your garden or terrace, or even if you don't have one at all, you can still grow a few herbs. The easiest ones to grow are the perennial ones – once planted they will keep on growing over a number of years. Parsley, Thyme, Rosemary and Mint are all good choices, but make sure that you put your Mint in a pot, not a garden bed or else it will take over everything in its path.

If you are lucky, Basil will come back year after year in a garden bed but once Coriander (Cilantro) dies down, that's curtains and you'll need to buy more.

Five Top Tips

1. For fresh flowers that last for ages, choose Orchids, Lilies, Chrysanthemums or Carnations

2. Read the little care tag that came with your plant – you can pretty safely assume that the person who grew it knows how to look after it

3. Clean a stained vase with hot soapy water and a bottle brush; for really stubborn stains, try a denture-cleaning tablet. (Steal it from your grandma!)

4. To do a simple vase arrangement, insert your foliage and then insert an odd number of focal flowers

5. To get a bud to open more quickly, put the flowers in warm water and gently pull apart the buds at the tip

With many thanks to Sophie Kempton for her help in writing this chapter.

FIRST IMPRESSIONS LAST

This chapter is about modern manners. You might think that etiquette is just a weird set of rules from a bygone era. Well, in a way it is but it's also all about being considerate of other people's needs and feelings. People will make judgements about you based on the way you behave, so read on to keep yourself nice.

Haven't Got Time To Read The Whole Chapter? Read This.

1. You will be judged by the way you behave. Stand out by being on time, writing thank you letters and being formal with older people

2. First impressions count. Make sure you look people in the eyes, have a firm handshake, remember names and show interest in other people

3. Cutlery is placed on the table in the order that it will be used, starting from the outside and working in. So your soup spoon will be on the outside of your knife, which will be outside your dessert spoon

4. When you are with others, leave your phone alone and in your pocket or bag. Don't read or write texts, don't sit your phone on the table, and let all calls go through to voicemail. Show your companion that they are more important than your phone – even if you actually prefer your phone

5. When a relationship breaks up, it's not reasonable to expect that you will continue to be friends. Leave the other person in peace, don't call them when you've had one too many and don't even think about break-up sex.

Want To Make Your Mark?

Want to stand out from the crowd (but in a good way)? Try these.

Be on time

If you organise to meet someone in a public place (such as a café or park) be there on time. Your friend will feel like a goose hanging around somewhere alone so don't be late. On the other hand, if you are going to someone's house, don't arrive bang on time – give them 10 to 15 minutes grace otherwise you might find your host in their underwear. (I'm not going to comment on whether that might be a good thing).

Be formal with older people

Be formal when you meet older people socially for the first time – call them Mr or Mrs. It might feel strange or make you feel like a suck, but it will mark you out as being respectful and polite. (And they will ask you to call them by their first name anyway, so there's no great loss). Don't do this at the office – it would just be weird.

Thank you letters

Isn't it a great feeling to get a handwritten letter in your letterbox? Whenever you can, write one. People love them. The letter itself doesn't need to be too flash but try to make it sincere and mention something about why you enjoyed the event or gift.

Having said that, it is also fine to send a thank you letter in the same format as you received the invitation. So, if you are invited somewhere by email then you can send a thank you letter by email; if you are invited by text it's fine to send a thank you by text. Try to do it within a couple of days of the event, although if you forget it's better late than never.

Holding open doors

Okay, controversial territory coming up! When you are walking with an older woman (say your grandmother or mother) or your female boss, and you are male, it is polite to let the woman enter through a doorway first. You should make an effort to open the door for her. You should allow her to enter a lift before you do and to exit before you do as well. It is not patronising but a sign of a man who knows what's what.

However, with a woman of your own age, be careful! Some women love it and even more so on a formal occasion; some see it as yet another sign of a patriarchal society at work.

Meeting People

Generally

Making a good impression can happen right from the very first time you meet someone. You should try to:

- Have a firm handshake – not a bone-breaker but also not one like a pathetic wet fish. The former says you are trying too hard; the latter is just off-putting
- Look people in the eye when you are talking to them. Don't be weird about it, don't invade their personal space and don't zoom in on them with radar eyes, but a bit of eye contact is a good thing
- Try to speak up and don't mumble. It's annoying if people have to strain to hear you
- Show interest in the other person. Ask them questions about themselves and see if you have any common ground. You never know, you might both be interested in local weavers of the Xinjiang Uyghur Autonomous Region
- Try to remember and use their name. Some people use a mnemonic. For example, say you meet an exceptionally neat woman called Christine – think 'Pristine Christine'.

Tips for meeting the parents (uh oh)

It can be really nerve-wracking to meet the parents of your current favourite person for the first time. No doubt you want to make a good impression, so try the following.

Checklist: Meeting the parents for the first time

- Dress smartly – depending on your gender, don't wear clothes that are too revealing or too casual
- Don't be late, and take a small gift such as a bottle of wine or some chocolates
- Turn off your phone before you go inside
- Shake hands and make eye contact (yes, this is appropriate too if you are a woman)

- Watch your table manners and eat whatever is offered. Your partner should have worded the parents up if you are unable to eat certain foods for medical, religious or ethical reasons (such as meat, pork or gluten). If there has been a slip up, accept the items on to your plate with no comment and leave them on the side of the plate discreetly
- Accept a modest second helping – this makes the cook feel that you really liked what they made
- Drink only a modest amount of alcohol – things can go wrong in so many different ways if you don't
- Show interest in younger siblings, pets, and any evident interests of the parents and be careful discussing politics, sex or religion.

Tips For Going Out

Replying to invitations

When you receive an invitation, try to reply to it within a week. (Yes, really!) Some invitations will have an RSVP date on them; in previous generations this was avoided as it implies that the people you are inviting do not know that they should reply quickly. Try not to use one in your own invitations. However, if you have dodgy friends, go ahead and put a date in!

You should reply in the same way in which you received the invitation. So, if you receive an invitation by SMS, reply by SMS. If you receive an invitation by email, reply by email. This means, of course, that if you receive a written invitation, you should reply in writing unless the invitation has an email address or phone number on it, in which case you can reply in either of these ways.

Bringing someone along

Unless you have a '+1' on Facebook, or your invitation says '& friend', then don't ask if you can bring someone along. Numbers at parties can be limited by finances or the size of the venue and it can embarrass the host to ask.

Being in control

When you go out, try to keep yourself nice! There's nothing worse than waking up the next morning and remembering what you did – or even worse not remembering what you did! Besides the obvious humiliation, you put yourself at risk in all sorts of ways, so don't drink or take other substances which cause you to lose control and embarrass yourself. Wait till you get home before you go wild.

Be inclusive

So, you're at a dinner and seated next to the man or woman of your dreams on one side and a boring old fart on the other. Be a good guest! Talk to them both for about equal amounts of time.

You will appreciate how good this advice is when you are next seated between two people who both turn their backs on you and talk to others all night.

Going to two parties on the one night

Don't go to two or more parties on the one night – it's not fair on the host who has tried hard to put on a good party and who is hoping it will be a great night. There's nothing worse than seeing half your guests disappear after an hour or so.

And which one should you choose? It's the one you were invited to first. If both invitations arrive about the same time, then you have the luxury of choosing the one you'd rather be at.

What To Wear?

Many invitations tell you what to wear and often this is pretty clear: there can be no doubt what casual means, and even Semi-formal is not too confusing. But there are some others which might be confusing and these include the following:

Lounge Suit

If you find Lounge Suit written on an invitation, for men this will generally mean a standard suit and tie, or a jacket (made out of a different fabric to your trousers) and tie. It's definitely not the same as Black Tie. For women it's pretty free-range, but something semi-formal would be appropriate.

Black Tie or Formal

What is very specific is the use of the words Black Tie or Formal. This means that the men should wear a black tie suit which consists of a black jacket with satin lapels, and trousers which have a thin satin stripe down the outside of each trouser leg. This is what is known as a tuxedo or 'tux' in the U.S. (Don't say this in Australia or the U.K. – it sounds like you spend your life watching old American sit-coms.)

The shirt you wear with black tie is a white one with a pleated front, and loose metal studs instead of buttons. You should also wear cufflinks and not buttons at the cuffs. The correct tie to wear with this is a self-tied black bow tie and never a clip-on tie.

It's worth noting here that it is becoming more acceptable for men to wear plain black suits with black ties (not bow ties) and white shirts instead of the full black tie gig at formal events.

Women have more choice and can wear full-length, maxi, or short dresses, but these should be formal in nature and designed for evening wear.

White Tie

White Tie is even more formal and means that a man should wear a black suit with tails (a 'penguin' suit), a white shirt with a textured front and a white textured waistcoat, a white cummerbund, and a self-tied white bow tie. For women, this would most likely indicate that they should be wearing a full-length (to the ground) formal dress.

At home

At home is an old-fashioned phrase that you may find on an invitation. It usually means a drinks party at (you guessed it) the host's home, and the title is more related to tradition rather than indicating anything about the event itself.

At a wedding

If the dress has not been specified as above then it can be tricky to know what to wear. Men can always wear a suit and women something semi-formal and all should be well. Traditionally, women should not wear black (too funereal) or white (looks like you're competing with the bride). You don't need to wear a hat any more but go ahead if it's a daytime wedding, particularly if it's formal.

At the races

The races give you an opportunity to go to town in terms of dressing up. Given that you will be walking around outside on grass in all sorts of weather, they are surprisingly formal. Men MUST wear a suit and women a hat (and probably something else as well). Go wild! It's the one time of the year that you can wear something outrageous and no-one will blink an eye.

Girls, make sure you dress for the weather, watch out for sunburn and don't wear your 10" Manolos. You're on your feet all day and alcohol might compromise your ability to walk in them.

On Derby day, women should wear black and white, the only day of the Spring Carnival that dictates the colour of your dress. Every other day you will have free rein (ha ha). Men on the other hand need to know which flowers to wear in their lapel on each day: a white rose for the Caulfield Cup, a Cornflower for the Derby, a yellow rose for the Melbourne Cup, a pink rose for Oaks Day and a red rose for Stakes Day. Try to source them from a friendly neighbour or your own garden – otherwise you'll be subject to once-a-year price-gouging from local florists. Be careful – if you get the flower wrong, you'll be seen as a newb – particularly at the Derby and the Cup.

At a funeral

I'm sure you know what to wear at a funeral – subdued (e.g. not a Hawaiian shirt or something fluoro), modest (not shorts, a sundress or a brief top) and appropriate (not sportswear). Men should wear a dark suit; women can wear what they like but it should be better than your average day wear. Women don't need to wear a hat. Arrive at least 30 minutes early or you may not get a seat, and make sure you sign the attendance book at the entrance to the church. The bereaved family won't remember who was there but they will be pleased to see your name on the register. And one last thing: if you are about to cross the road and see a funeral procession coming, you should stop and bow your head until it passes.

Wearing hats inside

Never wear a hat inside (and this includes the wearing of a hoodie with the hood up, or a cap) unless you are a woman and you are dressed formally, such as for the races or for a wedding. Otherwise, as soon as you walk inside you should immediately remove your hat.

Also, make sure you remove your sunglasses (and also your hat if it obscures your face) when you are outside and are talking to someone. It's just polite to let people see your eyes. Yep, that's just the way it is.

Going To Someone's House

Take a gift

When you visit someone's house, take a small gift. It doesn't need to be too flash and can be something simple and even better if it is something home-made or home-grown. Try a jar of jam or chutney, a small bunch of flowers from your garden, or a small container of home-made biscuits.

If you hear that someone is unwell, why not deliver some food to their house so they do not have to worry about cooking? A good thing to deliver is a quiche, as this is easy to transport, can be eaten hot or cold, and lasts for several days if they already have other plans. And after you look at the recipe section of this book, you will know how to make these things yourself!

When it comes to birthdays, don't go overboard on the gifts as this will make your budget go bananas. Again, why not give something home-made? This is more meaningful than something that you have just quickly bought on the way home from work.

Table behaviour

When you are at someone's house for dinner, don't start eating before the hostess (and if no hostess, the host) has started. If she tells you to begin before her, then go ahead, otherwise you need to wait until she is seated and has started eating before you begin. The hostess should also be the last person to finish eating, keeping other guests company while they eat.

Send a thank you

As mentioned earlier, make sure you thank the host or hostess the next day. If it's too hard to ring or write, a text is better than nothing.

Hosting Guests At Your House

Seeing people to the door

When someone arrives at your house, make sure you greet them at the door. Don't call out 'come in, the door's open'. Going to the door makes guests feel welcome. You should also walk guests to the door when they are leaving. Yes, right to the very door. And to their car or taxi if they are elderly. One other thing: make sure your outdoor lights are on if it's dark when they arrive and when they leave.

Introductions

Practice making good introductions. Always say the name of the person you are showing the most respect to first e.g. parents, grandparents, your girlfriend or boyfriend or your boss, and repeat the names. For example, you would say "Grandma, I'd like you to meet my friend Simon. Simon, this is my grandma, Mrs Smith." If introducing two people and you know you are going to have to leave them, it can be helpful to say something that they have in common e.g. "Andrea, I'd like you to meet Tim. Tim, this is Andrea. Did you know that you both play Royal Tennis?" Then they've got something to talk about when you disappear.

Table seating

The guest of honour (say the person whose birthday it is, or an overseas visitor) should be seated on the right of the host or hostess of the opposite sex, and will be served their meal first. The partner of the guest of honour will be seated at the right of the other host or hostess. So for instance, Will from overseas will be seated at the right of the hostess, Will's partner Jenny (or maybe it's Andy – doesn't matter) will be seated at the right of the host.

And…

And make sure the bathroom is tidy and the toilet is clean. Put away all your medication as that's no-one's business but your own. There should be a clean hand-towel, and a small bunch of flowers would be nice.

How To Set The Table Correctly

It can be confusing to set the table correctly, but here's a guide to make things easier.

Glasses

The shorter stemmed glass with the biggest bowl is the red wine glass, the taller stemmed glass with the smaller bowl is for white wine and the narrow taller flute is for champagne. The glass without the stem is for water.

Wine glasses and a water glass should be placed directly north of the cutlery on the right hand side of the setting.

Cutlery

Cutlery should be placed on each side of the plate, in the order in which it will be used, starting at the outside.

So, on the right hand side you will have (starting on the outside), the soup spoon, the entrée knife or pretty fish knife (if you are having an entrée or fish course), the main course knife and then the dessert spoon. On the left hand side you will have (starting from the outside), the entrée fork or fish fork, the main course fork and the dessert fork. Yes, there should always be a dessert fork when you are using a dessert spoon. Please note that although you will sometimes see this, particularly when you are out, it is not correct to place the dessert spoon and fork above the plate.

Table decoration

Make sure your table decoration is not so high that it will obscure vision across the table. If it is, remove it before you sit down (which pretty much defeats its purpose I'd reckon).

Pepper & salt

Make sure that your cruets (pepper and salt containers) are full. They should be placed in front of the guest(s) of honour and the salt should be on the right of the pepper. Okay – it's not so important but those who know will be impressed if you do it correctly! These, as well as any mustards or sauces, should be removed before the dessert course is served.

Table Manners

Holding a knife and fork properly

No one will tell you this, but people will notice if you don't know the correct way to hold your knife and fork, and this will indicate to them a lack of awareness of social niceties. In particular, please do not hold your knife as if it were a pen (what some people call a 'dear momma', as if you were writing a letter to your mother!). Your right hand should be on top of the handle, with your forefinger extended down to the very start of the top of the blade. This is the correct way of holding the fork in your left hand as well.

If you currently hold your knife and fork in the incorrect manner, please change it now. Yes, it's meaningless when there are such bad things that happen in the world, but why not make life easier for yourself? It's sad but I know people who wouldn't employ you if you held your cutlery the wrong way.

Picking up your food

Please never hold your food up – such as holding your bread in your hand while you spread it with butter. This is just not correct. And while we're at it, never hold your cutlery up either. Don't gesture with your hand while it holds a knife or fork. Unless you are trying to stab the waiter, that is.

Licking your knife

Someone as polite as you would never do this, would you?

Buttering bread

When you use butter, you should put it on the side of the bread and butter plate and not straight on to the bread. You should also break your roll or bread into a small piece, then butter it and eat it, rather than buttering the whole lot then eating it bit by bit.

You should also break bread and cut toast. Weird, hey? But that's just the way it is.

Napkin

When you sit down, unfold the napkin and place it on your lap unless a waiter does it for you. At the end of the meal, remove it and neatly gather it on the bread and butter plate. And here's a bit of trivia for you: cloth napkins are called napkins and paper ones are called serviettes.

Position of knife and fork

Sometimes during a meal you might want to put your knife and fork down, for instance, if you want to pick your nose. (Nah, only kidding, you can use your knife to pick your nose). Anyway, make sure that the knife and fork are placed in the position of an 'X', with the knife blade facing in and the fork crossed over the knife with the tines pointing down. Similarly the dessertspoon and fork should also be placed to rest on the plate in an 'X', with the spoon bowl facing up and the fork crossed over the spoon with the tines facing down.

When you have finished your main meal, place your knife and fork together in the middle of your plate, the fork (with up-turned tines) on the left and the knife (with in-turned blade) on the right. After the dessert course, you should again place your cutlery in the middle of the plate, with the fork on the left with the tines up-turned, and the spoon with the bowl up-turned on the right. If you still have food left on your plate, you should move it to the side of the plate, and then place your cutlery as above. Don't leave your cutlery resting in the food.

(And did you know that you should always leave a very small amount of food on your plate? If you eat it all it implies to the host or hostess that perhaps there was not enough food).

Serving from left, taking from right

Okay, you may have seen this on Downton Abbey. When you are serving food or drink to someone who is seated, you serve the food to the left, and the wine to the right. This means that if a wine waiter and food waiter are both serving at the same time, they do not bang into each other! Conversely, when you are removing the empty plate you remove it from the right-hand side. Simple.

Don't take it all

If you are helping yourself from a platter, don't take too much! For instance, if there are eight pieces of steak and eight people, don't take two. In addition, always take the food closest to you, even if it is less appetising than food further away on the platter. Don't take that tasty looking piece of steak on the far side of the platter, hidden under another piece. And finally, you should never, ever take the last piece of food on a platter, unless your hostess or host tells you to do so.

Mobile Phone

There's a whole lot of etiquette around using your mobile phone, but most of it relates to either not disturbing others, or not being rude to the people you are with.

Checklist: using your mobile phone

When you are with others:
• If you are in the middle of something (such as organising to go somewhere, or sending an important text for work), try to finish it before you meet your friends
• Turn your phone to silent and put it away. Don't put your phone on the table unless it's been invited to dinner too
• Give your full attention to your companion(s). Don't make a call, and let all voice calls go to voicemail. If someone's trying to reach you urgently (and to be honest – how often does that happen?) they will continue to ring
• Don't check your phone for messages, and don't write texts
• If you absolutely have to make a call or text someone, try to leave the table and do it in a discreet place. If that's just not possible, explain what you need to do to the people you are with. We've all got busy lives so everyone understands that sometimes you just have to get on with it.
When you are in a public place:
• Don't shout. You don't need to! Your voice sounds softer to you on a mobile phone than on a landline. Fun fact: with a landline there is amplification of your voice into the earpiece (this is called Side Tone) but mobile phones don't have it. This means your voice sounds louder to you on your landline than on your mobile. Also, due to a thing called Automatic Gain Control, which mobile phones do have, if you speak quietly, the signal is amplified and if you speak loudly it is diminished. (Thanks Dr Karl[62]!) For these two reasons you need to consciously practice speaking quietly on a mobile phone

- Be mindful of where you should avoid use of your phone completely e.g. a library, a lecture, the cinema or in church
- Never make shop employees wait when they are serving you. This is guaranteed to absolutely piss them off
- And above all, never drive and use your mobile phone. It's the law and besides, it's really, really stupid.

On-Line Netiquette

And there's also a few things to remember when you are on-line:

- Don't use capitals in your posts or emails. It's shouting WHICH IS RUDE AND DISTURBING, NOT TO MENTION THREATENING

- Be careful with your grammar and spelling. It says a lot about you. (And this is true in all your communications, not just electronic ones.)

- And have you ever received an email written at 3am and wondered what the person was doing up at that time? Be careful what time you are on-line because people will make judgements about you and your lifestyle

- Don't forward jokes unless you are sure the recipient will appreciate them. Some people might not appreciate your humour (hard to believe); others might just not want the extra volume in their in-box

- Tone is hard to judge on-line so be careful with what you write. It can be easy to misinterpret what someone has said

- And on the other hand, be forgiving – perhaps what you understood is not what they meant

- Don't write, post or send something that you don't want everyone to read. If it's something cruel, are you that sort of person? And do you really want the person concerned to read it one day? That photo – are you happy that it's starting a life out there on its own? And was that secret really yours to share?

- And furthermore, don't sext. Really? You didn't know that?

- If you are upset, or the topic is controversial, wait a while and have a think before you post or send it on its way. If you're writing an email and planning to think about it before you send it, leave the To: box empty. That way it won't be sent by mistake

- And finally, remember that there is always a person at the other end. Treat them with respect.

Relationships

Ending a relationship

If you need to end a relationship, don't send a text or just change your status on Facebook; be brave and do it face to face. It's not going to be pretty but once it's over you can be happy that you did the honourable thing. Whatever has happened in the past, don't tell your partner what they've done wrong or list their faults, as tempting as that might seem. Enough for you to say that the relationship is no longer working, that you wish them all the best, and that you hope you can still be friends. (Yep – everyone says that and it's nice, but accept that in reality it probably won't happen; it's hard to stay friends with someone who's dumped you.)

Try to leave your ex-partner in peace and avoid being there every step of the way in their grieving period. Treat them how you would hope to be treated in the same situation. And if you're the one who has been dumped, try to get on with your life and avoid any drunk-dialling. It's no good for anyone and it's really bad for your self-esteem next morning.

Break-up sex

No. No. No. Break-up sex is never a good idea as it can be confusing for both of you and may raise false expectations for the dumpee. Don't do it.

Five Top Tips

1. Reply to invitations as soon as you can, and certainly within a week. You should reply by the same method as which you were invited

2. It might be tempting, but don't go to two parties on the one night – it's not fair on the host. You should always go to the party you were invited to first

3. If you're a woman, don't wear black or white to a wedding

4. Don't ever wear a hat inside, unless you are a woman and it's a formal hat. If you're wearing a hat, take it off as you cross the threshold

5. Don't use capitals in your on-line communications.
   IT'S RUDE AND A BIT SCARY.

CHAPTER 14

OMG! IT'S AN EMERGENCY!

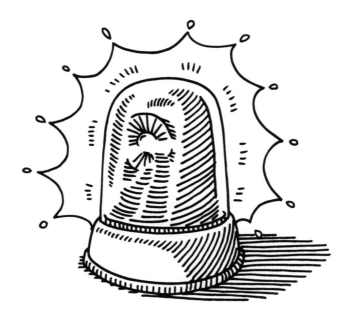

So life is cruising along quite happily, then out of the blue – disaster! Make sure you take a few basic steps beforehand so that if something crap happens you can recover from it quickly. And try to stay calm and follow the advice in this chapter.

Haven't Got Time To Read The Whole Chapter? Read This.

1. Keep a photocopy of all your valuable information including your cards and passport in a folder in a secure location. If you are in rented accommodation, keep a list of your rental agent's preferred repairers on the fridge as well as their out-of-hours emergency number

2. If you lose your phone, have a good look for it then immediately notify your supplier to avoid responsibility for any costs incurred by the person who's taken it

3. If you need to dial the emergency services, be prepared to say whether you need Ambulance, Police or Fire, make sure you know your address and the nearest cross-road, and don't hang up till they tell you to do so

4. To put out a cooking fire, cover the pan with a lid or a fire blanket and then turn off the burner if it is safe to do so

5. To make an insurance claim for a stolen item, you will need a police report. This requires a visit in person to your local police station in order to get one.

000 is the emergency call number in Australia; if your phone is out of range dial 112. The emergency number in the U.S. is 911, in the U.K. is 999 and in Europe is 112.

Checklist - Before an emergency

Make sure you gather all the following together and put them in a folder in a safe place:

- A photocopy of all your cards. This includes bank cards, licence, Medicare card, store cards, ID card, student cards and travel cards (such as Myki or Opal)
- A photocopy of other important documents e.g. your passport
- Your mobile phone's IMEI number (dial *#06# to get it.)
- Important phone numbers (gas, electricity, water, landline, rental agent)
- If you are in rented accommodation, a copy of the rental agent's preferred repairers and their out-of-hours emergency phone number
- Photographs of any valuables such as electronics, jewellery or decorative arts
- Receipts for purchases of insured items such as computers or TVs.

You should also:

- Make sure you know how to turn the water off
- Find out where the fuse box (for power) is
- Install a find my phone App on your mobile phone
- Test smoke alarms by pushing the little button with a broom handle once a month, and replace the battery once a year at the end of daylight saving. If you are in a rental property this should be done annually by the landlord or rental agency, but it's up to you to check.

What to do if you have a car accident

1. Check that all passengers are okay. If not, call 000 or 112 if out or range in Australia (or 911 in the U.S., 112 in Europe and 999 in the U.K.)

2. Move your car out of the way of other traffic, if it is safe to do so

3. Get the details of the other driver, their car and their insurance company (or take a photo of their licence and the car's number plate)

4. If there are witnesses, get their contact details as well

5. Take photos of any damage to either car

6. Ring your insurance company – they will organise a tow truck if necessary

7. Ring to see if a friend can come and help. If your car is driveable, they can drive you and it home.

What to do if you lose your wallet

1. Look for it everywhere you've been (ring around if you need to) as well as down the back of the sofa, in bags and in pockets

2. Tell your friends and family you've lost your wallet and ask them to look out for it

3. Take out the photocopy of your cards and start ringing the banks to cancel and re-issue them. Start with the ones that bear a financial risk (e.g. credit cards) and don't worry about ones like your Medicare card (no-one's going to go wild with that!)

4. Ask a family member or close friend if you can borrow some cash to see you through the next couple of days.

What to do if you lose your phone

1. Try to track it down using a find my phone App such as *'Find my iPhone'* or *'Wheres my Droid'*

2. Ring any recent destinations to see if they have it and ask friends and family. Check pockets and bags and down the side of sofas

3. If you have no success, report it immediately to your network provider who will block your phone. Don't worry – if you find it in the pizza box next morning, they will usually be able to reactivate it. This is really important (not the pizza box part, the blocking part) as you will be responsible for any bills until you let your provider know

4. If you have insurance that covers your phone, go to the local police station (don't call the emergency services) and report the loss. They will make a report, which you can then use to make a claim

5. Even if you don't find your phone you will need to keep paying for the contract until it runs out (yep, sad but true).

What to do if your phone stops working

1. Did you drop it or let it get wet? Go to a mobile phone repair shop and cough up for repairs. A screen can cost as little as $50 to repair

2. Has it just stopped working and you are under contract or still in warranty? Contact the place where you bought it to organise a replacement or repair

3. If your phone is still not working, the supplier won't help, and it's obviously a dud, contact the Telecommunications Industry Ombudsman (TIO) or go to the TIO website.

What to do if you've been burgled

1. Do not confront a robber. Only enter your place if you are sure it's empty

2. Call the police on 000 in Australia (or 999 in the U.K. 112 in Europe and 911 in the U.S.) and be prepared to give them your address and the name of the nearest cross street. If you feel unsafe, go and sit in a neighbour's place or your locked car till the police arrive

3. Do not touch anything – this is to avoid tainting the evidence

4. Once the police have been, start making a list of all things that have been stolen

5. Call your insurance company and report the burglary

6. Being burgled can be confronting, so be prepared to talk with someone about it.

What to do if the power goes out

1. Check if the neighbours have power. If everyone's power is out, you can relax as the power company will be on to it

2. If it's just your power that's out, ring your power supply company

3. Try to avoid opening the fridge or freezer as they can warm up quickly

4. If you are going to bed with no power, make sure you have turned off the lights and other appliances otherwise you could get a big fright in the middle of the night when the power comes back on!

What to do if you have no water

1. Check if the neighbours have water. If everyone's water is out, wait an hour or so. If it's still not on, ring your water supply company

2. If it's just your water that's out, ring your water supply company

3. Remember that toilets don't flush without water, so be stingy with your toilet flushing (gross but practical)

4. Make sure that if you turn on taps to test if the water is working, that you turn them off again.

What to do if you have a flood

A broken pipe

1. Turn off the water supply to the house

2. Ring your water supply company if the pipe is outside your house and call a plumber if it's inside your house.

A broken appliance

1. If it's from a broken appliance such as a dishwasher or washing machine, turn off the water supply to the appliance

2. Mop up the mess

3. Call a friendly repair man or woman.

From a sudden downpour

1. Check that there is no blocked drain or gutter causing the problem

2. Ring your neighbours for help

3. Grab all the towels you can and make a barrier so that the water can't enter into the whole house

4. Grab brooms and mops and sweep the water out of open doors

5. Make sure that you keep the water away from a power source, such as power points or leads. If in doubt turn off the power at the switch box.

What to do if you have a fire

Stovetop or oven

1. If the fire is in a pan, cover it with a well-fitting lid or fire blanket. Slide the lid in from the side rather than dropping from the top to avoid burns. If the fire is in the oven or microwave, shut the door

2. Turn the oven or burner off as long as you can do so safely

3. Wait till everything cools down before opening the door or moving the pan

4. If the fire gets out of control, exit the house and call the Fire Brigade.

Clothing

1. Drop down to the ground and roll. Cover your face with your hands

2. If possible, get someone to throw a woollen rug over you

3. Keep rolling till the fire goes out

4. Treat burns by cooling in running water for 20 minutes, and seek medical advice if the burns cover a large area or are very painful

5. Take a painkiller.

House fire

1. Escape from the house by crawling low (that's where you'll find the least smoky air)

2. Shut doors behind you if you can to slow the movement of the fire (but remember they can have hot door handles)

3. Call the Fire Brigade once safely outside

4. Wait outside and don't be tempted to go back in to get any valuables.

What to do if there is a medical emergency

1. Make sure the surrounding area is safe and that you will not be in any danger by going to help. Watch out for electrical danger

2. See if the patient is responding by gently shaking their shoulder and talking to them

3. If there is no response, call the emergency number and ask for an ambulance. Stay calm, be prepared to give your location and don't hang up till they tell you to do so

4. Follow instructions from the operator. Their advice will include checking the patient's airways and breathing, and starting CPR

5. Keep going until the ambulance arrives or the patient recovers.

What to do if you are burnt

1. Immerse the burnt part in cool running water for 20 minutes
2. Do not apply anything else such as aloe-vera, cream or ice packs
3. See the doctor if the burn is very painful or covers a large area
4. Take a pain killer.

What to do if you cut yourself

1. Apply pressure to the area with a clean pad (such as a tea-towel)
2. Elevate the part above your heart and keep calm
3. See a doctor if you can't control the bleeding or the cut is very deep.

What to do if you are attacked

1. If your attacker is after property (such as your phone or wallet), give it to them
2. If they are trying to hurt you, be loud, scream, cause a fuss
3. Make every effort to escape to a safe place
4. Only fight as a last resort as it can inflame the situation
5. Once you are safe, go to the police to make a report
6. Seek psychological support from a trusted source.

If you have been sexually assaulted in Australia, call 1800 737 732 for free, confidential, 24/7 help. They will put you in contact with a service close to where you are.

What to do if you are broke

1. Take a deep breath and face the situation. It won't go away by itself but you will be able to sort it out
2. Go and get advice from a financial counsellor. There is often free advice to be found at uni, on your local council's website or at the Human Services[63] website. Some companies also employ a counsellor who may be able to help
3. Ring the people you owe money to and explain the situation. Reassure them that you are willing to pay, but are in a difficult position
4. For the short-term, can you sell something? Do some extra part-time work around the neighbourhood?

5. Talk to your friends – they may have advice or help to offer, or at least a shoulder to cry on.

Five Top Tips

1. If you have a car accident, photograph the other person's licence and car number plate, as well as the damage to both cars

2. Keep a copy of your mobile phone's IMEI number. If you don't have it, dial *#06# to get it

3. If the power has gone out and it's time to go to bed, make sure you turn off all your lights and radio to avoid a rude awakening in the middle of the night

4. To put out a fire in your clothes or hair, drop to the ground and roll

5. To stop bleeding, apply pressure to the cut with a clean pad and elevate the part above the heart. Keep the patient calm.

Footnotes

Chapter 1

[1] http://www.consumer.vic.gov.au/housing-and-accommodation/renting

Chapter 2

[2] *Proof of Identity (100 point check)* Human Services, Aug 2012.

[3] http://www.apca.com.au/policy-and-debate/public-consultations/decline-of-cheques

[4] http://www.datagenetics.com/blog/september32012/

[5] http://au.pcmag.com/password-managers-products/feature/4524/the-best-passwordmanagers

[6] https://agilebits.com/onepassword

[7] http://www.veda.com.au/insights/comprehensive-credit-reporting-ccr

[8] http://www.asx.com.au/documents/resources/getting_started_in_shares.pdf

[9] https://www.ato.gov.au/Individuals/Lodging-your-tax-return/Lodge-online/e-tax/

[10] https://www.ato.gov.au/calculators-and-tools/do-i-need-to-lodge-a-tax-return/

[11] http://www.legalaid.vic.gov.au/find-legal-answers/wills-and-estates/making-validwill

Chapter 3

[12] https://www.moneysmart.gov.au/tools-and-resources/calculators-and-tools/budgetplanner

[13] http://www.bigoven.com/recipes/leftover

[14] http://www.choice.com.au/reviews-and-tests/household/energy-and-water/savingenergy/standby-energy.aspx

[15] http://www.goget.com.au

[16] http://www.scamwatch.gov.au

[17] http://www.lost.amta.org.au

[18] http://www.humanservices.gov.au/customer/services/centrelink/financialinformation-service

Chapter 4

[19] www.linkedin.com.au.

[20] www.jobs.com.au, www.seek.com.au or www.careerone.com.au

Chapter 5

[21] http://lowfatcooking.about.com/od/healthandfitness/a/nonstickpans.htm
[22] www.taste.com.au[23] http://www.bigoven.com/recipes/leftover

[24] *Franklin, P. Plastic water bottles should no longer be a wasted resource,* Container Recycling Institute http://www.container-recycling.org/index.php/issues/bottledwater/275-down-the-drain

[25] http://www.webmd.com/food-recipes/features/cookware-plastics-shoppers-guideto-food-safety?page=2

Chapter 6

[26] *2011, Supermarket Health Eating for Life (SHELf) protocol of a randomised controlled trial promoting healthy food and beverage consumption through price reduction and skill building strategies.* Deakin University. With thanks to Kylie Ball

[27] Jack Purcell Meats: www.jackpurcellmeats.com.au

Chapter 7

[28] *Sexually Transmissible Infections.* Australian Social Trends, Australian Bureau of Statistics, June 2012.

[29] 2013, National Health & Medical Research Council *The Australian*

Dietary Guidelines

[30] http://www.measureup.gov.au

[31] AIHW 2014. *Australia's health 2014 — in brief.* Australia's health no. 14.
Cat. no. AUS 181. Canberra: AIHW.

[32] AIHW 2014. *Australia's health 2014*—in brief. Australia's health no. 14.
Cat. no. AUS 181. Canberra: AIHW.

[33] June 2012, Australian Bureau of Statistics, Australian Social Trends
Sexually Transmissible Infections

[34] http://www.humanservices.gov.au/customer/forms/3170

[35] www.comparethemarket.com.au

[36] *Young Person's Oral Survival Guide,* Australian Dental Association

[37] http://darta.net.au

[38] www.Ambulance.(nsw, vic or qld).gov.au, www.saAmbulance.com.
au, esa.act.gov.au/actas

[39] http://www.druginfo.adf.org.au

[40] http://www.counsellingonline.org.au

Chapter 8

[41] Suiter, D. Toews, M. and Ames L., *Stored Product Pests in the Home.*
UGA Extension, 2014

[42] Choe, D, *Clothes Moths.* Pest Notes, University of California, March
2013.

Chapter 9

[43] Ellery, B. *Ice in six out of ten restaurants has more bacteria than water from
toilets,* The Daily Mail Australia, 2013

Chapter 10

[44] www.mynrma.com.au

[45] http://www.ancap.com.au/starratings

[46] *Global Status Report on Road Safety 2013.* World Health Organisation , 2013.

[47] http://www.ancap.com.au/safetyfeatures

[48] www.howsafeisyourcar.com.au

[49] Newstead S & D'Elia A, *An investigation into the relationship between vehicle colour and crash risk.* Monash University Accident Research Centre, 2007

[50] http://www.raa.com.au/motoring-and-road-safety/car-advice/converting-your-carto-lpg

[51] http://www.raa.com.au/motoring-and-road-safety/car-advice/converting-your-carto-lpg

[52] E.g. www.carloans.com.au

[53] http://www.consumer.vic.gov.au/motor-cars/buying-a-used-car/ways-to-buy-aused-car/private-seller

[54] To register your car have a look at:
ACT www.rego.act.gov.au/registrations/regomain.htm
New South Wales: http://www.rta.nsw.gov.au/registration/index.html.
Northern Territory: http://transport.nt.gov.au/mvr/about-us in NT
Queensland: http://www.tmr.qld.gov.au/Registration/Registration-fees-andlabels. aspx
South Australia: http://www.sa.gov.au/subject transport,+travel+and+motoring/motoring/vehicles+and+registration
Tasmania http://www.transport.tas.gov.au/registration_information
Victoria: http://www.vicroads.vic.gov.au/Home/Registration/
Western Australia: http://www.transport.wa.gov.au/licensing/20414.asp

[55] Such as http://www.rta.nsw.gov.au/licensing/downloads/road_users_handbook.pdf

[56] http://www.beaurepaires.com.au

[57] AAMI, *Annual Road Safety Index.* 2011

[58] For further information, look at your licence handbook or get on-line

and go to:
ACT http://www.rego.act.gov.au/infringements
NSW http://www.rms.nsw.gov.au
QLD http://www.qld.gov.au/transport/
SA https://www.sa.gov.au/topics/transport-travel-and-motoring
TAS http://www.transport.tas.gov.au
VIC http://www.vicroads.vic.gov.au
WA http://www.transport.wa.gov.au

Chapter 11

[59] http://kb.rspca.org.au/What-do-I-need-to-know-before-I-get-a-new-pet_19.html

[60] http://www.ava.com.au/news/media-centre/hot-topics-5

[61] 2013 *Domestic Animal Management Plan 2013-2017* City of Stonnington

Chapter 13

[62] Kruszelnicki, Karl S. *Shout while speaking on mobile* ABC Science, 2014.

Chapter 14

[63] www.humanservices.gov.au

Index

To order another copy of this book, please go to

www.movingoutbook.com.au

Made in the USA
San Bernardino, CA
27 December 2019